As author Sandra Felton states: "Because we are made in God's image we desperately want to look at our own creation and say that it is good."

Are these lies keeping you from creating a beautiful and orderly home?

Lie: Being Messy is a superior way of life.
Truth: "When the house is messy and our lives are disorganized, we lose touch with what is peaceful and noble in ourselves, and our self-image suffers."

Lie: Messies need more willpower and discipline.
Truth: "Messies need focus, not fogginess."

Lie: Working harder will keep your house clean
Truth: "You already work hard enough! You have to uncover the underlying causes."

Lie: I'm a hopeless Messie.
Truth: "Getting a house under control requires nothing that we do not have or cannot get. You have an orderly person within you."

Let these and countless other truths transform you into a *Messie No More!*

MESSIE

NO

MORE

BY Sandra Felton

Meditations for Messies
Messies Manual
Messies 2
Messie No More
Messies Superguide
Messies Calendar

MESSIE

NO

MORE

Sandra Felton

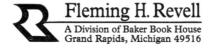
Fleming H. Revell
A Division of Baker Book House
Grand Rapids, Michigan 49516

Copyright © 1989 by Sandra Felton
Published by Fleming H. Revell
a division of Baker Book House Company
P.O. Box 6287, Grand Rapids, Michigan 49516-6287

ISBN: 0-8007-5302-X

Tenth printing, November 1993

Printed in the United States of America

Illustrations by Louise Bauer

Printed in the United States of America

Help. I am lost. Return me to:

Initials:

Address:

CONTENTS

ACKNOWLEDGMENTS

I WOULD BE REMISS if I did not mention the help I received from the teachers and librarians at Hialeah High School. These learned women lay me in the shade literarily. Any references I have needed and leads I have asked for they have given me. Through their conversations in the faculty lounge, they have unknowingly been my advisors.

No one knows but I the value of the inspiration and information I receive from people attending my seminars and workshops and from others I meet. Many offer perceptive comments and exhibit courage that is invaluable to me in sharpening my understanding of the importance of organization in women's lives. From them I have gained a better understanding of the need to live with dignity and effectiveness and to use our qualities to the fullest extent.

Special thanks to Bob Schwartz who wrote *Diets Don't Work*. His understanding of the search for normalcy in the area of weight control has been a great help to me in understanding my search for normalcy in the area of order in the home. He and I met once as guests on a television show, and if I had known then what I know now about his book I would have thanked him in person—many times.

THE AUTHOR

I AM A MILD-MANNERED schoolteacher who is certified in math and in special education. As I write this I am teaching special education English in high school. In the mornings and at night I write. On some weekends I go into a phone booth, put on my Superwoman outfit, and fly off to various parts of our great country to hold seminars or to speak to women's groups on the subject of organization in the home. With the help of two others I oversee Messies Anonymous, a program I founded to help Messies through seminars, books, newsletters, and self-help groups.

Of my three children, two young adult sons still live with us in our small Florida home. My daughter, our oldest child, lives with her husband, cats, and horses in rural Georgia, where she teaches elementary school.

I could not keep the schedule I do without support from others, most of which comes from my husband, Ivan, who is a minister and is doing his best to bring order and beauty to the spiritual area of people's lives. The members of our church are understanding, and they offer much in the way of personal strengthening just by our gathering and their love.

Do not think that I am a dynamo of energy. Nothing could be further from the truth. My energy level is low. I do not run a tight organizational ship. The only reason I am able to do all I do is by exercising moderation. My balanced life does not get out of kilter when one thing goes wrong because it is not so tightly packed that one error messes everything up.

I set goals for myself, but I limit them to a few. Then I head in that direction, forgiving myself when things go wrong and going on with a casual attitude.

When I look around every so often I usually see that I have accomplished more than I realized I was doing.

INTRODUCTION

NOTHING IS MORE FRUSTRATING than being required to do something beyond our ability. Those of us who call ourselves Messies live daily with the reality of this problem. We want to keep the house in order and beautiful. But many of us find it next to impossible to do so.

There are many examples of this kind of problem, but perhaps none illustrates the situation better than the story of Rumpelstiltskin.

The miller in the story had a shrewd and clever daughter and boasted to the king that she could spin straw into gold. The king loved gold, so he locked the girl into a room filled with straw and ordered her to perform her miracle.

Rumpelstiltskin learned that the beautiful miller's daughter had been asked to do the impossible, and he took advantage of the situation. Appearing miraculously through the locked door, he promised to spin the straw into gold if the girl would give him her ring.

She agreed, knowing it was the only way she could save her life.

But the king was not satisfied with one roomful of gold. He brought in another load of straw for the miller's daughter to transform. Again Rumpelstiltskin appeared, this time demanding the girl's necklace as payment.

Still not satisfied, the king demanded the young girl to work her magic for a third time. Rumpelstiltskin appeared again, but this time he demanded the girl's firstborn son.

Messies can sympathize with the miller's poor daughter. Many Messies are bright and creative. Because of this, people expect them to be able to perform simple housekeeping chores without any problem. We expect it of ourselves. But it seems as impossible for us to do this as it was for the miller's daughter to spin straw into gold. Neither threats nor promises move us toward success. We wish for a little elf to come in and do the job for us, but he never arrives.

This book is the next best thing. It won't clean your house for you, and it doesn't come with coupons for maid service, but it will help you develop the mindset that makes messiness a thing of the past.

Many who are reading this book are desperate to change and don't know how. Many have tried various methods and slipped back into old habits. Some keep things picked up but at a great price of physical and emotional effort. They have improved, but find it hard to keep up. Many of these strugglers feel very much alone. Quietly, doggedly, daily, they fight the clutter, which, like the tide, is constantly coming in. Their husbands may be urging them to do better. Their children may be embarrassed. They may feel like failures because they can't get things moving in the right direction. Whether their house is terribly messy or just consistently more cluttered than they want it to be, they feel that it is out of control no matter how hard they work to control it.

Most of us know how to do more than we are doing, so this is not another "how to" book. It does, however, contain many practical ideas geared for Messies. It has some information your mother never told you (or she told you when you weren't listening). All of it will help you move toward the goal of order and beauty in your life. But it only works when you are mentally and emotionally ready to work at it.

In this book you will discover the reasons your house is out of control. Then you will learn ways to get things back under control and keep them that way. I know it sounds too good to be true, but it's not. Your friends and neighbors who are not neat freaks don't have cluttered houses, do they? They don't even seem to be interested in housekeeping. How do they do it? What is their secret? You're about to find out.

This book contains the basis for a permanent change. In its own way, it is the foundational book of the Messies Anonymous program. It requires some written participation that is essential for accomplishing your purposes. Your written responses are an important part of the changes you will make.

If you don't want anyone to know what you are reading, cover the outside and write "The Total Watercress Health Diet" or some such inane thing across the front. That should keep folks out.

I am an eclectic reader, so I draw material from many— sometimes unlikely—sources. Like a butterfly sipping from one blossom and then another, I do not check the type of soil each flower is growing in. In other words, when I refer to an idea or quote an author I am not necessarily endorsing the overall philosophy. I leave it to the readers' good judgment to discern those things for themselves.

This book is the fourth in a series. The other books are *The Messies Manual*, *Messies 2*, and *The Messies SuperGuide*. Each has a place in bringing the message of hope to Messies who feel hopeless.

MESSIE

NO

MORE

Part 1

WHY?

Understanding the Messie Mindset

THE SECRET TO CHANGE lies in the way we think about messiness and neatness. Somewhere in this section you will find yourself and your way of thinking. Not all types will apply to you, but you will discover some destructive thought patterns that are so much a part of you that they seem normal. They are an important part of your housekeeping problems.

Many women keep neat houses without becoming compulsive, and it's because they think differently from the way you do. You will find out their secret and learn to make it your own.

1

ACCEPTING YOURSELF

Messiness & All

T HE GOONEY BIRD is funny-looking. When it walks it has to lift high its large webbed feet to keep from tripping over them. It also engages in a strange-looking courting ritual. Gooney birds bow and stretch in front of each other. Their large, round bodies are awkward on land, where they court, lay their eggs, and raise their young.

The albatross, on the other hand, is one of the most graceful birds in the world. It has a wingspan of up to twelve feet and can glide on its long thin wings longer than any other bird. It is both beautiful and regal.

Few people realize that the gooney bird and the albatross are the same bird with different names. On land it is the gooney bird, ungainly and inept. In the air it is the albatross, king of the sky.

Messies are like this bird. In the area of organization we are at our weakest, floundering in our attempts to be neat. Like the gooney bird, we have no way to avoid functioning in our weak area. But like the albatross, we do have our sky. Messies function beautifully in many ways, soaring easily in our areas of strength.

As we struggle to improve in the organizational area, we can find satisfaction as we soar in other areas.

Messies, however, usually don't see the beautiful side of themselves. All they see is the gooney bird. And they don't like what they see. As a result, Messies treat themselves badly. They're not very nice to themselves, not very nice at all. This is not evident at first, however. Messies are vibrant people who seem to participate in life to the hilt. They are very particular about their personal belongings, and to an extent they are particular about themselves as well. Many of them appear to be happy, well-adjusted people.

Further examination, however, brings another underlying pattern to the surface. In hundreds of ways a day Messies, because of the way they think, treat themselves like second-class people.

For Messies, much of life goes on in the mind, so they don't like to be bothered with the day-to-day details of life. As a result, they put up with dripping plumbing and broken appliances because getting them fixed is too much trouble. They live without enough light in strategic places because correcting the problem is more of a bother than living with it.

On the other hand, Messies always have good intentions. They keep old clothes, convinced that someday they will mend or update them. They have stashes of greeting cards they purchased but never got around to sending.

Messies are forgetful, so they keep everything out where they can see it. If they put it away, they know they'll forget to do it. They blow their noses on toilet paper instead of tissues because they keep forgetting to buy Kleenex. They have too few clocks, mirrors, and trash cans because they never think to buy them.

Messies are perfectionists, so they live in clutter and chaos because there's never enough time to do everything according to their high standards.

Messies are impulsive, so when they decide to bake something special at the last minute they rarely have the ingredients the recipe calls for.

Messies are impatient, so they use salt, pepper, and sugar from the containers they are purchased in because transferring them to salt and pepper shakers or a sugar bowl takes too much time.

In hundreds of ways Messies do without. The old-fashioned way of doing things, so popular with Messies, is just another systematic way of doing without modern conveniences or supplies.

People's lives have dark places as well as bright ones, difficulties as well as abilities....
The combination makes us unique.

In the light of this daily denial of what they need to make life comfortable, it is not surprising that they also deny themselves a place to sit on the sofa because it is covered with stuff. They deny themselves companionship because they can't invite guests over with the house the way it is. They sometimes sleep on the floor because the bed is piled with clothes they haven't had time to put away.

But Messies are used to self-denial. They do without or make do. Instead of recognizing the problem, they live without. And they are very good at it. Many even take pride in their make-do approach. They are happy to show you how they do without the things people who recognize their worth and dignity provide for themselves.

Ultimately Messies deny themselves a life of serenity and beauty. They insult themselves with disorganization on such a regular basis that they are unaware of it. The messy house is just part of a picture of a person who consistently abuses herself. Messiness is just the top of a very deep pile of problems.

The First Step

To put an end to this pattern of denial, Messies must first stop fighting themselves. If we get angry at ourselves and go to war against certain character traits every time we see them, we only give them the energy to stay. *Star Trek* fans may remember the story called "The Empath" in which Mr. Spock and Captain Kirk were surrounded by a force field that kept them from helping Dr. McCoy, who was in trouble. The more they struggled to get out, the stronger the force field became because it gained strength from the energy of their struggle. When Mr. Spock realized this and stopped struggling, the force field lost its power to restrain them.

Like Mr. Spock, the more we struggle against the force that holds us back, the stronger the force gets. Unless we accept ourselves and our habits and our lives *as they are* NOW we will never overcome the negative forces.

You may be angry at yourself, the house, or the thoughts that got you in this fix when it first dawns on you what has been happening. Don't fight the anger; it is part of the picture too and must be accepted. And it will pass. It generally has a short life span. When it has done its work, we can get back to self-acceptance.

I cannot overemphasize the importance of self-acceptance. We are people of dignity. We love order and beauty. We are worthwhile. Zig Ziglar tells of a painting by Rembrandt that sold for over a million dollars. Ziglar wondered why the price was so high. Is paint that expensive? Does canvas cost a lot? Of course not. The value of the painting was twofold.

1. It was painted by a master.
2. It is one of a kind.

This story reminds us of our own value. We were painted, shadows and highlights, by a Master Painter who "does all things well," who made both the albatross and the gooney bird parts of us. We are wonderful because we come from his hand.

Like Rembrandt's painting, we too are unique. No one else has our exact makeup, our strengths and weaknesses, shadows and highlights. Rembrandt's paintings have a lot of shadow in them, but it enhances their beauty. People's lives have dark places as well as bright ones, difficulties as well as abilities. It is fine to have both. The combination makes us unique.

Why Not?

Most of the time when I talk to people about Messies Anonymous they know only too well why someone would want to change her house. Occasionally, however, on a radio talk show or in an interview for a newspaper, someone will ask why people should be concerned about getting their houses in order.

My best answer to that question is another question—Why not?

Why not have a lovely home that encourages all who enter? Why not be among those who are thrilled to invite people on the spur of the moment? Why not be the person to whom people say, "Your house is so lovely!" Why not have people over for meals without working yourself to death to get ready? Why not have a house that raises your self-esteem rather than tears it down? Why not have a house filled with your favorite colors and accents? Why not have a house that reflects the peace and grace of God so that others love to come over to hear about Him? Why not have a house in which you can read or pray without feeling guilty because you're not cleaning? The question is not why should we have a nice house. The real question is WHY NOT?

Assess the Mess

1. List all the ways you deny yourself, even those you think of as frugality. They will not all come to mind at once (you may be so used to living with them that none come to mind at all), so turn down the corner of the page so you can find it easily to add to the list. (Yes! the corner of the page. Yes! I did say turn it down. I know it may bother you to mess up the book, but you will be writing in it anyway, so it won't matter.)

a.

b.

c.

2. If money were no object, what things around the house would you upgrade? What would you buy that you have been denying yourself? Jot them down quickly and add others as you recognize changes that you would like to make.

   a.

   b.

   c.

3. List your characteristics, both albatross and gooney bird, that combine to make you unique.

   a. (albatross)

   b. (albatross)

   c. (albatross)

   d. (gooney bird)

   e. (gooney bird)

   f. (gooney bird)

4. Why do you think Messies deny themselves?

2

WHY YOU ARE MESSY

The Saver

IF YOU DON'T WANT IT, give it to Susan. She takes everything.

It's true. Susan hates to see things go to waste, and she's sure she'll find a use for the things, at least most of them, someday. So her basement, attic, garage, and every spare corner are crammed with things no one else wants. Susan's not sure she wants them either, but she doesn't dare get rid of them. If she throws something away, she is sure she will need it the next day. And besides, it's too late to start saying no to people's offers. They might think she is ungrateful. What's a saver to do? Buy a bigger house?

Susan's obsession with saving comes from her desire to always have whatever she or anyone else ever needs. Her mentality is not uncommon, but it's only one of the many mindsets that leads to uncontrolled saving.

Messies have very real reasons for doing what they do. And they feel very strongly about their reasons. Messies are generally logical and intelligent people. Although they may not like a disorganized life and the problems it causes, the things they do that keep it that way are consistent with how they think.

Messies have problems in three basic areas: saving too much, cluttering, and wasting time.

As we look at these areas in the next three chapters put a check beside the thinking patterns that fit you.

Saving

☐ 1. **Scarcity**. Messies live on the verge of the next Great Depression. An article on "Pack Rats" in *Psychology Today* confirms that people who save too much are not just those who lived through the depression. Many people who have always lived in affluence hoard things because they fear, emotionally if not intellectually, that they will not have enough in the future. Is this a factor in your thinking?

☐ 2. **Hobby**. Some people so love saving that they specialize in it. Wealthy people do this with art or other collections. People of ordinary means love to collect too. They collect bottles, antiques, figurines, etc. It gives them something to talk about, something to do on vacation, and puts them in contact with friends and acquaintances they would not otherwise have. Messies collect too many things, the wrong kind of things, and just junk. They are pack rats. Does collecting affect your house negatively?

☐ 3. **Comfort**. Some Messies find comfort in having a lot of belongings. They feel better when they have boxes, bottles, papers, clothes, and food around the house. Perhaps things are so out of order that having many of the same item gives them some assurance that they will be able to find at least one when they need it. Do you find comfort in things?

☐ **4. One-of-a-kind things**. Some things are unique, so we reason, "If I don't buy this rabbit-shaped butter mold now I may never see one again. If I want it, I had better get it." Have you ever done this type of gathering?

☐ **5. Guilt**. Benjamin Franklin did much to set the tone for saving. *Poor Richard's Almanac* is full of catchy sayings about it. His admonitions have followed us through the history of our country. Certainly wanton wastefulness is a bad idea. So is wanton saving, but nobody has made a slogan about that. What sayings have you built your life on? Two that are applicable to our situation are "Waste not, want not" and "A penny saved is a penny earned." What other slogans have set the stage for your overcollecting? Do you ever feel guilty for getting rid of things?

Wanton wastefulness is a bad idea.
So is wanton saving,
but nobody has made a slogan about that.

☐ **6. Bargains**. The mantel clock was such a bargain she had to get it. Only a fool would pass up such an opportunity. But she didn't have a mantel—or any other place to put it. Do you buy things you don't need simply because they are cheap?

☐ **7. Gratitude**. They may be birthday or wedding gifts from relatives or secondhand junk from a friend, but they have two things in common: they are free and they are associated with someone we love or care about. This makes them impossible to part with. They appeal to both our frugality and sentimentality. We feel that we have to take them and, what's more, that we have to keep them. Do you have difficulty getting rid of useless gifts?

☐ 8. **Sentimentality.** Messies are afraid they will forget the past. Many do have poor memories. They need to be able to touch and hold things from the past to keep it alive. Messies take multiple pictures, sometimes compulsively, to capture the present for posterity. Do you save to keep the past alive?

☐ 9. **Anthropomorphism.** No one except a Messie can fully understand the feeling that "things" have a life of their own. The life they have is usually part of the life of the person who owned them. If I get rid of something meaningful to me I feel as if I am giving away part of myself. Even worse, if I get rid of something that has belonged to someone meaningful to me, I feel that I am giving away part of them and betraying their memory. It is more a feeling than a thought.

When you acquire things
that don't satisfy your need,
no amount is ever enough.

When it came time for me to give away my last maternity dress, I put it on the bed each day so it could lie in state. I needed to do that to get used to the idea that it was going to leave my house *and* for *it* to get used to the idea that it was leaving. When Messies get rid of something, they often feel they must find a good home for it and check up on how it is getting along. This is difficult to do, so we decide it is easier just to keep the things. Do you sometimes feel that things have feelings?

☐ 10. **Fear.** "What if the I.R.S. should audit? I need to keep everything I might ever need!" It is true that everyone needs to keep records for tax purposes, but the reality is that if we keep all the stuff we're afraid to throw away we won't be able to find the old income tax forms, much less the receipts and records that go with them, if we ever need them. We are afraid we will need receipts for the credit cards or for the department store or the light company or something. It is certainly a good idea to have what we need for these occasions, but the unreasonable fear that causes us to keep too much is as much trouble as keeping too little. Do you keep all records just in case you will be asked to produce some of them sometime? Have you ever needed them?

☐ 11. **Procrastination.** Some Messies put off getting rid of things that require action. Every day the mailman delivers a new batch of problems for Messies. They don't want to pay the bills until the due date, so they let them pile up. They don't want to take the time right now to read the junk mail, so they keep that. They want to save the magazine for a more relaxing day, so they save that. After only a few days they have a box full of "to do" reading. Then the boxes start piling up.

A procrastinating Messie told me that he wishes for a fire to get rid of the clutter. That way he could blame God, not himself, that some things never got done. Does procrastination cause clutter in your life?

☐ 12. **Value.** It's not right to get rid of things that have worth. Books and magazines contain valuable ideas. The pen is mightier than the sword. Messies believe that they have power at their fingertips in this printed material. It doesn't matter to them that some of those textbooks are so old that the ideas are long outdated. Nor does it matter that most of the books are packed away and they don't know where they are and can't remember what's in them. Their value is more imaginary than real.

Messies are incredibly hopeful when it comes to the future value of things. They fervently hope that some obscure item will become valuable. They even imagine the wild stories the neighbors will tell their children when it happens. "See that house over there. The person who lived in it kept almost everything he ever owned. One day in his basement he came across a mint-condition, first copy of a Superman comic book. That thing brought two million dollars at an auction. Now he's moved away to a mansion. He used to be as poor as a church mouse. Now he's on easy street. I sure wish I had been as wise as he was and kept everything I ever laid my hands on."

Many Messies collect things for the same reason others buy lottery tickets. They hope one day to strike it rich. Are you collecting because you think your items have or will have great value? Are the things you collect worth the trouble of living with them?

☐ 13. **Posterity.** There is a great temptation to keep things for the grandchildren. "They don't make toys as good as the ones I bought for my children. What a thrill for little Billy to play with the bulldozer his dad had at his age." And on it goes. Are you keeping things for posterity?

☐ 14. **Mother-of-the-world.** For reasons discussed later in the book, Messies feel responsible for the whole world's well-being. If no one else in the neighborhood has something, we think people should be able to come to us and get it. We save old catalogs just in case a neighbor's child needs to get pictures for a school poster. The little kid who wants scrap wood for his project can find it at

Messies collect things for the same reason
others buy lottery tickets.
They hope one day to strike it rich.

our house. Why don't these kids' folks have the things they need? Because they are providing an orderly and clutter-free home so the kids will be spared the confusion that exists at ours. Do you think you have to have something in case someone else needs it?

☐ 15. **Habit.** We have gotten so used to keeping things that we no longer bother to make a choice about them. If someone puts a flyer on our windshield, we keep it. If we are sent a coupon in the mail, we keep it. The kids bring home stuff from school. We keep it all. When we receive a letter we even keep the empty envelope. With few exceptions, we keep everything that comes to our hands. It is our way of life. Do you keep things without thinking about whether or not you really need them?

☐ 16. **Creativity.** Those who perceive themselves as creative like to find creative uses for junk. They cut up a bleach bottle and use it to hold clothespins on the clothesline. They cut off the feet of ruined panty hose and fill them with soap slivers for bathing. And they save things they don't have a use for just in case they might think of one. They don't know what to do with all their old butter tubs, but they are "too good" to throw away.

I once caught myself wanting to save the underwires that I had removed from bras. I thought about painting them and making Christmas ornaments. Now really! Who wants bra underwire Christmas ornaments! Or bra underwire anything. But such is our desire to save for creativity. It is part of the Messie's make-do mentality. Do you have the creative urge to make things from junk?

☐ 17. **Rebellion**. If someone got rid of your things when you were a child, perhaps you keep stuff to show that you now have power over your own things. In this case, the more your mom or husband urges you to get rid of things, the more determined you are to keep them. Now that you are grown up, you can clutter to your heart's content and no one can stop you. Are you a rebellious clutterer?

☐ 18. **Satisfaction**. Some people try to get from their belongings something that belongings can never give. Because people are unfulfilled and cannot find satisfaction, they keep gathering more and more stuff, hoping that one day it will satisfy them. But it never does. Look at the word *fulfilled*. It means "filled full." They think that if they get filled full enough they will feel fulfilled. The truth is, when you acquire things that don't satisfy your need, no amount is ever enough. Are you looking for satisfaction in the things you save?

☐ 19. **Holidays.** The holidays are times of overdoing. People overeat, overbuy, overcelebrate, and overwork. It is not surprising that many people also overdo on holiday collecting. The stores are full of decorations that convince us we need every one. Collectors reason that they can pass them to their grandchildren if they get too many. This kind of collecting is hard to resist for sentimental Messies. Do you overbuy during the holidays?

"I can't seem to chip away at my own junk buildup," wrote Roberta Katchen Stein in the *Chicago Tribune* (July 29, 1984). "I cling to my backlog of possessions as zealously as Peter Pan stuck to his shadow."

If you and your possessions are inseparable, it's time to reassess your situation.

Assess the Mess

1. List the factors mentioned in this chapter that cause you to save too much. Add any others that you have thought of.

   a.

   b.

   c.

   d.

2. Give examples of how they affect you.

   a.

   b.

   c.

   d.

3

WHY YOU ARE MESSY

The Clutterer

CONNIE LEAVES PILES of clothes all over the house. It used to drive her mother crazy, then her roommates, and now her husband. They are all amazed that she manages to look good whenever she goes out. They can't figure out why she doesn't always look as if she just crawled out of the dirty clothes hamper. But there's a method to Connie's madness. What no one understands is that it's the piles that *keep* Connie from looking that way. They are her way of sorting her wardrobe. Since she's slightly perfectionistic, she can't bear the idea of putting once-worn clothes back in the closet where they might contaminate the clean clothes. But neither does she want to put them with the dirty clothes because she might have to wear them again before she does the laundry. So the piles work well for Connie. Anything in a pile is still wearable, and on laundry day all she has to do is pick up the piles and tote them to the laundry room.

There are, of course, more sensible solutions to Connie's dilemma, but because no one understands the way she thinks, no one can help her. And, of course, there are many other reasons why people clutter their surroundings.

☐ 1. **Poor memory**. People who have a poor memory are afraid to put things away because they will forget where they are or even that they have them.

☐ 2. **No place to put things away**. The house is small, storage space is scarce, and there is already too much stuff in the storage places. In short, the stuff is spilling over because there's too much of it. Messies find it difficult to know what storage pieces are needed, and they don't think of buying things like cabinets and shelves. Their make-do mentality is one of the reasons they have no place to put things.

☐ 3. **Energy conservation**. Messies believe in production-line straightening. We don't put away one little thing at a time. We let things pile up. Then we gather them into similar groups and put everything away at the same time. While we are waiting to start the assembly line, the house is a wreck.

☐ 4. **Serendipitous helping**. Somewhere, sometime the clutterer heard a story about someone who was united with long lost relatives through a set of unlikely circumstances. Perhaps a friend was visiting a clutterer who had snapshots lying on the lamp table. The friend glanced at a photo and said, "That man looks like my uncle,

Bernie Stein, who was killed in Germany during the war." "Why, that's Sam Stein!" the photo owner says. "He and his dad, Bernie, run a deli in Miami Beach! Bernie isn't dead! He's alive and well!" The clutterer is thrilled that he has helped reunite these family members. And it was all because he left out his snapshots.

☐ 5. **To keep people away.** The cluttered house is an excuse to keep people out. When our house is too cluttered to entertain, we have a reason for not allowing visitors to use up our time. Even though some disorganized people want to entertain, they find it very difficult to do so.

☐ 6. **Love.** We love to see our nice things. Why should we put them away?

Messies believe in production-line straightening. But while we are waiting to start the assembly line the house is a wreck.

☐ 7. **Distractions.** The distractible person starts a job and then quits, leaving a bunch of stuff undone. She puts something down without realizing it and doesn't remember where. She means to straighten things but something else comes up. Distractibility is a major contributor to messiness.

☐ 8. **Defines personality.** Being a Messie has certain advantages. One of them is that it makes us unique. We can make jokes about clutter. Others can tease us about it. We tell ourselves that being messy is a superior way of life. It is part of our self-concept. Some of us have signs on our desks (usually buried) that say, "A clean desk is a sign of a sick mind."

☐ 9. **Defines relationships.** Messiness plays an important part in some relationships. The messy person takes the place of the child even if she is an adult. Her mother, mother-in-law, husband, roommate, or some other figure takes the place of the parent. The messy person and the "parent" establish part of their relationship around the person's messiness. The "parent" fusses at the child. The "child" rebels or is sorry. Or both. The relationship is a negative one, but it is one they both understand. If the messy person were to change tomorrow, how would they relate?

☐ 10. **Attracts attention.** Occasionally the messy life-style gets much wanted attention. Well-meaning friends help us clean. They suggest ways of improving. All of this attention would disappear if the messiness disappeared.

☐ 11. **Family problems.** People who live in cluttered houses probably aren't the only clutterers. If they begin to live a clutter-free life there is no telling what conflicts might arise in the family. Other family members will want to continue leaving their shoes in the living room and their books on the dining room table. They already complain about having to put away a few of their things. Some people live cluttered lives to keep from upsetting the family.

Assess the Mess

List the factors mentioned in this chapter that contribute to your habit of cluttering. Add others that you have thought of. Give examples of how they affect your life.

1.

2.

3.

4.

4

WHY YOU ARE MESSY

The Time Waster

TAMMY, LIKE MANY MESSIES, is an optimistic person. One of the reasons for her optimism is that she has a very poor sense of time. She always underestimates how long it takes to do things. For twenty years it has taken her an hour to get ready for work in the morning. Nevertheless, every morning she optimistically thinks she can cut the time to forty-five minutes "if she just hurries a little bit," so she sleeps an extra fifteen minutes. But every morning for twenty years she has been fifteen minutes late for work. Because she is always running late, she never has time to put the breakfast dishes in the dishwasher, straighten the bathroom, or hang up the clothes she decided not to wear. Tammy has one of the classic characteristics of a time waster.

1. **Poor sense of passing time.** Many Messies have no sense of how long it takes to do things. When they agree to do something they do not realize they are humanly incapable of accomplishing it in the prescribed amount of time. Some don't even wear watches. They are not concerned about the timing of things, only about the doing. If they are distractible as well, they do not feel the flow of time in the way a non-distractible person does. The constant misjudgment of time is a sure symptom of the Messie mindset.

2. Sense of importance. Important people are busy people. They pack their schedules full to assure themselves of their own importance. People sometimes kill themselves with the idea that they are very important people doing very important work. A minister who had had several heart attacks but continued to keep a horrendously heavy schedule told a class of young seminary students that he was going to burn out for God. The pride with which he told the story led the students to wonder if he were not burning out for his own ego's sake. Sometimes our motives may surprise us.

3. Unwilling to take control. Some people are addicted to having others tell them what to do. They rarely schedule anything for themselves or decide anything for themselves. Instead, they "go with the flow" by waiting for parents, spouses, children, or God to tell them what to do. This leads to chaos because everyone has a different idea about what the Messie should be doing. We all have plenty of pressure without adding to it by allowing others to take control of our lives.

A favorite theme of C. S. Lewis is that only lazy people work hard. The unwillingness to make decisions about our own priorities and values is a form of laziness, and it results in a frantic life of always trying to meet the many demands to which we have haphazardly opened the door.

Sometimes Christians even take a sort of ouija board approach. They set up a system of signs for God and expect Him to show His guidance according to their rules. Perhaps it is God's will for them to set up their own thoughtful schedules and stick to them.

Knowing Makes a Difference

Knowing why we keep too much stuff, leave things around, and schedule our lives poorly is the first step toward change. Only when we realize what thoughts are guiding our actions can we begin to counteract them. To change our actions, we must change our thoughts. Many of the thoughts that guide our lives are good thoughts. They just don't work in our situation. Others are reasonable if not taken to the extreme to which we take them. And some are not as good as we thought when we first embraced them.

Only lazy people work hard.

At the circus you may see a 6,000-pound elephant tethered to a small stake with a thin rope. With his great strength he could easily pull the stake out or break the rope, but he doesn't know he can. As a baby, the elephant was strongly tied to an immovable object. He tried and tried to get loose but never could. Finally convinced that elephants tied to a stake cannot get loose, he stopped trying. Even though he is perfectly able to get away now, he doesn't try anymore. He lives by an idea he got a long time ago. It no longer applies to his situation but he sticks by it anyway. If someone who knew elephant talk would whisper to him that he doesn't have to live by the idea he got as a baby, do you think he would throw over his old idea? I think so. If he could see the life possible for him, I think he would choose freedom.

Most of our beliefs were set by the time we were twelve years old. Why are we willing to continue living by the beliefs of a twelve-year-old? Now that we are adults and know the ideas that motivate us to be messy, we can evaluate them and decide what we want to do with them.

Assess the Mess

List the factors that cause you to waste time. Add any of your own that you have thought of. Give examples of how they affect your life.

1.

2.

3.

4.

5.

5

A.D.D. ADDS

TO THE PROBLEM

LET'S FACE IT. Some kids are born disorganized. Nobody taught them slovenliness, but they are experts. Their scatterbrained behavior leaves the family in turmoil. Everybody thinks that if such children just cared more and tried harder they could improve, and all the adults have methods to motivate the mini-Messie to orderliness.

Mary's room is always a shambles. Her mom redecorated it, hoping Mary would care more about the room and keep it neat.

Little Johnny regularly forgets to turn in his homework. Actually, he doesn't forget; he can't find it. It's in his book bag or locker, he thinks. If you could see the book bag you would know why he's not sure. The family takes a "you're going to live with the consequences of your actions" approach after trying everything else. They believe that if he fails once he will be cured forever.

Ronny's mom sends him to the store to buy something only when she cannot find anyone else to go. All the time he is gone she wonders: Will he lose the money on the way? Will he remember what he went for? Will he lose the change or the package on the way home? Will he meet a friend and forget to come home at all?

All over the country children like these, through no effort or fault of their own, are driving their parents and teachers crazy. What the parents may not realize is that these children are more baffled than the parents about what the problem is. To the child the situation looks much different.

Mary's room, though a shambles to her mother's eyes, is not offensive to Mary's. She hardly notices how it looks and so she has a hard time understanding her mother's concern. As a matter of fact, when her mother points out the messy condition, Mary has a hard time understanding how it got that way. Whenever her mother gets the room straight, it seems to disorganize itself the minute Mary walks in.

Johnny's book bag and locker are a shambles. Nobody, not even a responsible adult, could use them successfully. His classmates have divider notebooks and are very neat. Johnny's papers are wrinkled masses amid his jumble of books. How his classmates keep things in order is a mystery to him. Being organized looks like a wonderful way of life, but he feels it is beyond his ability. His teachers and parents tell him it is easy and necessary to use a divider notebook. His father even bought one and set it up for him. But it wasn't long before the notebook was lost and his papers were again crumpled in the corners of his locker and book bag.

Ronny is keenly aware that he loses things, but he doesn't know why. It seems to him that people must be taking his things or moving them around secretly. When he leaves something out on a table, it disappears without a trace and he does not know where it went. Sometimes the item never comes back, and sometimes it reappears as mysteriously as it left. His parents, who are on his case about keeping up with his things, do not realize that all of this is confusing, frightening, and frustrating. Ronny has no control over his things and he doesn't know how to get control. His things seem to have a life of their own. His parent's hassling just adds further stress to this already stressful situation.

---

*Teenagers with A.D.D. are at higher risk
for depression and suicide.*

Teachers say these children need self-discipline. Psychologists say they need motivation. Doctors say they are immature. Parents oscillate between all three evaluations and their own despair. In the meantime, the offending children are trying to find a way to live in this confusing world. It may seem to others that they don't care, but this is usually not true. It's just that caring doesn't bring any relief. It just adds to the stress. So they go on as best they can. Sometimes their parents do help them by setting up an organizational system that alleviates the problem somewhat. Sometimes they compensate well, but for most the general problem remains the same. It doesn't help when adults treat them as though they are dumb or bad. Sometimes the children believe the adults may be right.

Children like these all over the country may be suffering from attention deficit disorder (A.D.D.), a term that has come into common use since about 1980. Previously, such terms as hyperactivity and minimum brain dysfunction were used to describe difficulty with concentration and attention span. There are two varieties of A.D.D.: with hyperactivity and without hyperactivity. In both cases the child is distractible (daydreams and has trouble ignoring distractions while trying to do a task), has a poor attention span (doesn't finish jobs or stick with them to the end), is impulsive (acts, talks, or makes decisions without thinking or self-restraint), and has poor social sense (has trouble making and keeping friends because of inappropriate behavior). Those who have hyperactivity in addition to A.D.D. are excessively active.

What Is Wrong With These Children?

Experts estimate that about 7 percent of the population has A.D.D. More boys have it than girls at a ratio of about nine to one. Experts believe it is caused by a problem with chemicals in the brain called neurotransmitters, which coordinate and regulate functions and behaviors. A slight deficiency in these neurotransmitters can cause the lack of attention that is a characteristic of A.D.D. and leads to messiness and disorganization.

A.D.D. tends to run in families. A child with A.D.D. usually has a parent or relative who has it. It does not seem to be related to head injury or any trauma at birth. Some have said that diet plays an important part in the problem. In this group are people who say that food additives are the culprit; others say that vitamin or mineral deficiencies cause it; still others relate it to allergic reactions. Although diet may be a factor in A.D.D., experts disagree as to the effectiveness of dietary regulations in controlling it.

Another factor in A.D.D. may be a problem relating to the muscular and neurological function of the eye. Just as some children (and adults) have responded to dietary change, some have responded to visual training by an optometrist who is a visual specialist. These approaches work with varying effectiveness and may be considered when a person is looking for help in managing this problem.

Sleep disorders also seem to play a part in A.D.D. Bed-wetting, grinding of teeth, and sleepwalking or talking may be indications of a sleep disorder. These disorders are more common among the A.D.D. population than the general public. One theory is that people who do not experience the natural sleep cycle, including the proper REM sleep cycle at night, must tune in and out during the day to get what other people get at night. The daytime symptoms of a person with a sleep disorder are similar to the symptoms of A.D.D. How sleep problems relate to A.D.D. is unclear and will require further study.

Since A.D.D. is a neurological problem with a biological basis, medication plays an important part in the solution. Medication increases the production of these chemical neurotransmitters and makes them more efficient. Parents of children with A.D.D. would do well to ask the child's doctor to recommend a child psychiatrist familiar with A.D.D. and its medical treatment.

Getting Through the Teen Years

As A.D.D. children reach puberty, the developmental lag tends to close. The problem seems to solve itself to some degree. But it does not solve itself completely. There remain some of the A.D.D. characteristics of distractibility, poor attention control, impulsiveness, and sometimes immature social behavior.

Teenagers have a hard enough time with new distractions in the areas of physical and social development and self-esteem. A teenager with attention deficit disorder can be expected to have a more turbulent time than most. Teens with this problem have had many negative experiences because of their own confusion about the condition and because of the misunderstanding of other people. Teenagers with A.D.D. have a higher incidence of academic problems, social problems, problems with drug and alcohol abuse, and even trouble with the law. As a result, they are at higher risk for depression and suicide. Problems with messiness and disorganization are just two of the many complications of A.D.D.

The A.D.D. Adult

As the A.D.D. child matures into adulthood, some residue of the disorder remains. Some of the problems that made the child disorganized and messy remain with the adult. The problem is compounded, however, because the life of the adult is so much more complex than the child's.

Sometimes the problem does not surface until the child becomes an adult. Mann and Greenspan, writing in the *Journal of Psychiatry*, say that the disorder is difficult to diagnose in an adult.

We suspect that many children with either mild or moderate attention difficulties, coupled with an unusual degree of creativity, intelligence and capacity for interpersonal relationships ... do not experience manifest psychiatric difficulties until they encounter the stresses of adult life.

This is why many women who have been able to hold their lives together through childhood and the teen years begin to falter when they have their own home and family to care for. Some falter after having one child, some after two. Each has a different level of ability depending on the severity of her A.D.D.

I faltered immediately after college. Until that time I was a little scatterbrained and spacey, but I got good support from home because it was always organized. I could handle my college schedule and my college room. But anything more than that (home, husband, work, children) was too much, as I found out immediately.

Keeping a house in order is a gargantuan task for a person with this disorder. Here are some examples of how it interferes with orderliness.

1. **Poor attention span**. Luci begins a large task, such as the week's laundry. She loads the dirty clothes into the car, drives to the Laundromat, lugs the full baskets to the washer, starts the washer, removes the clothes when they are finished, puts them into the dryer, and removes them when they are dry. By now she's had enough of the laundry. While her counterparts patiently fold their clean sheets, towels, and underwear and hang the shirts and dresses, Luci stuffs hers into the basket and goes home. She's had enough of one job for a while. But now she will have to iron the clothes that would have been wrinkle-free if she had hung them up straight from the dryer.

The same thing happens when she buys groceries, cooks, or starts a hobby. She has enough attention to get started but not enough to finish. So the one thing that usually goes undone is the cleanup.

These fears—losing things, forgetting things, not finishing things, doing the wrong thing, doing nothing—all cause more work.

Luci might tackle a big job like cleaning a large closet and run out of attention right in the middle of it. She leaves the mess in the middle of the floor for her husband to throw back into the closet when he gets tired of seeing it. Now the problem is bigger than it was before.

2. **Distractibility**. Dorothy is constantly pulled away from jobs by the telephone, her children's needs, and her own daydreams or interests. She works all day but accomplishes little because she does not go very far in any direction. Knowing she is distractible, she fears that she will forget to do something important.

To counter this tendency she leaves things out to remind her to do them. On the hall table is Joey's progress report she must sign and return to school. By the front door is the package she wants to mail and the can of food she wants to take to church for the food basket. On the dining room table are several bills to pay and some flyers she wants to look at.

She also does one thing while thinking about another, which causes forgetfulness. She will be so deep in thought that she will not notice where she puts things or remember whether or not she handled them at all.

Dorothy walks off and leaves the kitchen a mess after fixing a sandwich because she is distracted by the food she is going to eat. She may also leave the stove turned on and walk away. She writes a check and forgets to record it because the clerk distracts her. This amount of distractibility causes a chaotic, disorganized life.

3. **Impulsiveness.** Irma makes decisions too quickly. In a fit of neatness she throws something away, but a week later she needs it.

On a train trip from Florida to Indiana I had a stopover in Memphis, where I decided to clean out my purse. By mistake I kept the empty ticket envelope and threw away the envelope with the rest of my ticket in it. Not until I was on the moving train and the conductor came for my ticket did I realize what I had done.

This happens frequently to impulsive people. Unfortunately, instead of teaching them to be less impulsive, these bad experiences teach them to be hoarders. To keep from throwing away something they may someday need, they throw away nothing.

It is not just impulsive decisions to throw away things that cause problems for A.D.D. people. When they make a wrong decision as a result of impulsiveness, they learn to not make a decision again. This creates an inertia that leads to procrastination. For instance, an A.D.D. woman may want to attend a workshop but she never gets around to registering because she doesn't know for sure that she will be able to go. Maybe something else will come up. Maybe she already has an obligation she has forgotten. Maybe it costs too much. So she waits until she can be sure, and then it's too late.

Sometimes she doesn't hold back the impulsiveness. In a moment of inattention she does something inappropriate or blurts out things that embarrass her.

Two dangers constantly threaten the world: order and disorder.

Paul Valery

In the back of her mind is the ultimate fear that she will do something really dangerous. A North Carolina photographer and sky diver jumped out of the plane with his fellow sky divers and began to take pictures of them. But when it was time to pull the ripcord he realized he had jumped without his parachute. He was killed on impact. This kind of story frightens people who know they may someday make an impulsive decision of a serious nature. Sometimes this fear keeps them from making any decisions at all.

All of these fears—losing things, forgetting things, not finishing things, doing the wrong thing, doing nothing—cause more work. And because no one can do all this additional work, our families get angry, people put us down, and our self-esteem plummets.

The A.D.D. Struggle

A self-acknowledged Messie from Ohio wrote her observations about the inability to organize. Notice the similarities to the attention deficit disorder we have been discussing.

We Messies are probably victims of a neurological impairment. We cannot take in the larger picture. We are bogged down in details. We do not live on the surface; we are under a heap of impenetrable events, objects, people. We are baffled all the time about which is the next task. To say we struggle valiantly would be an understatement. No one could try more earnestly to make order out of chaos, but it is always just beyond us.

If we were limping along with crutches
people would understand that we have an impairment.
But we look and act so normal....

To give a specific example, when I have mustered an incredible amount of courage and have invited guests for dinner, I make lists, shop, and clean well ahead of time. I am a 69-year-old wife with nothing to distract me except one wonderful husband. My situation is the very finest any Messie could ever encounter. Yet, there always come the final moments of preparation when I panic—there is too much! It all needs to be done immediately, if not sooner. One thing at a time will never do it! There is nothing for it but to get on my horse and ride off in all directions at once, NOW. Things fly, get spilled, table cloth gets spotted, gravy gets dumped in sink as I try to strain out the lumps, etc.

If we were limping along with crutches, people would understand that we have an impairment. But we look and act so normal in most circumstances that no one can comprehend that we are battling just to stay at the same place—getting ahead is out of the question. Yes, it is funny. But if you could feel my heart racing and my breathlessness at the moment when inability lies exposed, with all seriousness I say you would see it is a bit tragic. The best way to describe my state at such times is to say my brain is scrambled, totally disorganized.

Probably Glenn Doman [a well-known neurologist] could have cured my disability had he been around in my childhood. But who would have recognized it? And had they, who would have considered it of much consequence? I function. But life is definitely harder for messies.

We are not a total loss, however. More than an ordinary percentage of us are musicians, artists, journalists. Our minds are seldom on the ordinary tasks we are doing, but are solving the world's woes. That is why we have to leave everything out in plain view that we do not want to forget. This is why we have to make endless lists (which we often lose). It is a rather miserable existence but our spirit is unquenchable! Dare I say the world would be a poorer place without us?

No more humiliation needed, so I won't sign my name.

Is There Any Help?

Although some A.D.D. symptoms diminish with age, adults still carry the confusion and fears of those early years. But adults have the advantage of knowing what is going on, which can keep them from kicking themselves around for being lazy, stupid, or disinterested.

The same treatments that apply to children with A.D.D. apply to adults. We cannot diagnose A.D.D. in ourselves. Diagnosis must be done by knowledgeable and experienced mental health professionals or physicians. Although A.D.D. is a difficult problem, it can be controlled through medication prescribed by a physician and with careful attention to contributing factors, such as visual problems, diet, and sleep disorders. Short-term psychotherapy may be appropriate, but a publication from the Minirth Meier Clinic reports that psychotherapy without medication seems to be ineffective.

For information on A.D.D. write to Minirth Meier Counseling Center, Collins Street, Richardson, TX 77873.

For information on sleep disorders (especially bed-wetting) write to Pacific International, Ltd., 555 Birch Street, Nekoosa, WI 54457. Or call (800) 826-5875.

Assess the Mess

1. Do you notice a particular number of A.D.D. characteristics in your own experience? List them.

   a.

   b.

   c.

2. Were you considered scatterbrained as a child? Write down an incident that stands out in your mind.

3. Have you had a particularly upsetting experience with lack of attention span, distractibility, impulsiveness, or poor social sense as an adult? Explain.

4. How have these characteristics

   a. affected your housekeeping abilities?

   b. influenced your personality and self-esteem?

6

COMPULSIVE

OR JUST MESSY?

WHEN DOES THE PROBLEM of messiness become the larger problem of compulsion? How can we tell whether we're just disorganized or whether we have a compulsive character style or a more serious problem called an obsessive-compulsive disorder?

Children with A.D.D. or adults with a personality disorder tend to become compulsive, to have an addictive personality. In an article in *Psychology Today* ("Against All Odds," December, 1985) the writer concludes:

> Addiction is a mysterious and complex phenomenon.... However, certain groups of traits, which are also characteristic of antisocial personalities, are seen in many types of addicts.... These include sensation-seeking, a short attention span, hyperactivity, emotional hypersensitivity and inability to delay gratification (absence of impulse control). When combined with a loveless early environment, these qualities often lead people to become compulsive....

We are well acquainted with the problems of addiction to alcohol and other drugs. We are also familiar with addictions to shopping, eating, gambling, and child abuse. Self-help groups have sprung up to address these disorders. In a related field, we are familiar with phobias such as the fear of heights, of flying, and of the outside world. All of these addictions, phobias, compulsions, and obsessive behaviors have been widely written about. Although they are not the same, they are similar in that they have to do with losing control. In all the writing about these disorders, however, little has been said about the disorganized life-style, although in its extreme it is an officially recognized obsessive-compulsive disorder.

A few parts of the problem have been addressed. For example, procrastination, hoarding, and chronic tardiness get some attention. But little or nothing is written about the lack of neatness, loss of important documents, perfectionistic cleaning compulsions, over-sentimentality that makes everything sacred, or the love of books and magazines that forces us to be priests of the god of knowledge. Many of us are paralyzed in these important facets of life, yet few seem to notice our grief.

Messies do not publicize the problem. For a woman, her house is an extension of herself. From our earliest days we associated the house with our mothers and what they provided. Women are nest builders. It is said that even animals do not foul their own nests. But Messies do. This says ugly things to a woman about herself. So like everything else, Messies hide this secret in the closet and, with everything else, they leave it there.

Not everyone who is messy has an obsessive-compulsive disorder. Dr. Harvey Milkman, professor of psychology at Metropolitan

State College in Denver, gives some guidelines to determine whether you may be approaching a serious problem with compulsion.

1. **Denial.** Does your family complain about the house and your part in it? Do you deny that you have a problem? (Does the statement, "Something has got to be done about this place! This is driving me crazy!" sound familiar?)

2. **Compulsion.** You have tried to change but you can't. You want to be neat, stop procrastinating, and stop saving, but it's somehow beyond your power.

3. **Loss of Control.** You are more and more drawn to the behavior. You do not have the time, energy, or will to stop.

4. **Progression.** Life has gotten less and less satisfying. You feel you cannot go out because you have work to do at the house. You can't invite others over without working yourself to death to get ready or letting the housework go and being embarrassed. More and more you are losing things and forgetting appointments.

---

*Compulsive people—both messy and neat—
are trying to gain control of a world
that seems to be very much out of control.*

---

5. **Withdrawal.** When you try to change you find that you have altered patterns of sleep, eating, or social interaction. If you try to get rid of things or challenge your perfectionism, you become depressed or upset. It frightens you to think of doing things differently.

If you answered yes to three or more, Dr. Milkman says you are on the road to a behavioral addiction or you are already there. People are drawn into these addictive types of behavior to enhance their own coping devices. We have all seen pictures of the homey farmhouse approach to decorating. Pots and pans hang from the rafters. Bric-a-brac adorns the shelves. Messies personify the homey approach run amuck. We fill spaces long after reaching the stylish point. We end up with junk. People hardly recognize that we were trying for the homey look. We have all of our papers and memorabilia, somewhere, and someday we will look at it, if we stumble across it before we die. In short, Messies take good and normal activities and overdo them.

Normal Activity	becomes	Compulsive Activity
Frugality ...		saving things unnecessarily
Sentimentality ...		obsessive hoarding of items from the past
Foresight ...		keeping every scrap "just in case"
Caution ...		paralysis from fear of making mistakes

Frequently we get so caught up in these activities that we fail to notice the toll they take. When people write to me about their struggles, they often mention drowning or they draw a picture of themselves drowning in clutter. A drowning person is caught in something deadly. Drowning is the ultimate lack of control.

Not everyone who drinks becomes an alcoholic. Not everyone who gambles gets hooked on it. Not everyone who diets becomes bulimic or anorexic. And not everyone who saves, clutters, or procrastinates becomes compulsive about it. But why? The answer is far from complete but a number of facts are known.

Low self-esteem is the cornerstone of addiction. The causes of low self-esteem relate mainly to the development of a faulty self-image in childhood, which can be caused by a number of things. We know there is an abnormally high incidence of sexual trauma in the background of women with addiction problems. Many have unhappy childhoods. Some studies indicate that adult children of alcoholics are more prone to addictive problems of all types. In *Guide to Recovery: A Book for Adult Children of Alcoholics*, Herbert L. Gravitz and Julie D. Bowden, founding members of the National Association for Children of Alcoholics, write, "Children of alcoholics are at maximum risk of becoming alcoholics themselves or developing other addictive behavior."

As mentioned earlier, those with A.D.D. are more prone to compulsion. There has been little research on the personalities, motivation, or psychological aspects of the lives of compulsive Messies.

Stanton Peele, author of *Love and Addiction* and *The Meaning of Addiction*, says, "A person will be predisposed to addiction to the extent that he cannot establish a meaningful relationship to his environment as a whole, and thus cannot develop a fully elaborated life. In this case, he will be susceptible to a mindless absorption in something external to himself."

Compulsive people—both messy and neat—are trying to gain control of a world that seems to be very much out of control. This feeling of control brings comfort, which is a precious commodity in a stressful world. Always present, however, is the overriding fear of losing control.

Of course, there are other factors at work as well. Genetics, peer pressure, and cultural influences all play a part in whether or not a person becomes compulsive. As an example, there are more female bulemics and anorexics than male. There are more male compulsive gamblers than female.

Men explain their addictions in terms of choices. They become addicted to things they want. Women explain their addictions in terms of feelings. They become addicted to things they love. Men tend to become Messies for practical reasons. They keep junk cars in the yard to use for parts that are hard to find. Women, on the other hand, become Messies for personal reasons. They feel an attachment to their belongings. They love their books, their sewing, and the like. They keep them to sustain personal satisfaction.

Much has been said about addiction or compulsion. Some people have multiple compulsions. *Health* magazine (October, 1987) reports that 59 percent of compulsive people have multiple obsessions. In *The Compulsive Woman*, Sandra Simpson LeSourd tells of her struggles with alcohol, smoking, shopping, overeating, overexercising, and other compulsions. Many compulsive people report that overcoming one problem just makes room for another.

Compulsive people tend to overdo in many areas. Lynne, a compulsive shopper and a member of Debtors Anonymous, says of herself, "Sometimes I wonder if I have an addictive personality. Like, recently I started to lift weights—maybe I'll overdo that now.

But I like to think a person can just change. If you have self-esteem and you know who you are, maybe you won't have to define yourself through extreme compulsive behavior" (*Ms.*, February, 1987).

Where can a person find the change Lynne was looking for? Whether or not you are a truly compulsive Messie, you will find help in following some of these paths to recovery.

1. **Admit the problem**. This is perhaps the hardest part. Some Messies can hardly face the idea of giving up the life-style that has been so much a part of their lives.

2. **Get help**. Join groups that address the basic self-esteem problem or join a Messies Anonymous group geared toward motivation and education. Perhaps therapy with someone familiar with compulsive problems will get you started on the road to recovery. Promising new medications are available to treat some types of obsessive-compulsive disorders.

---

*Knowing our intrinsic value tempers
our compulsion to prove who we are
through extreme behavior.*

In *The Compulsive Woman*, LeSourd gives eighty pages of references of help for compulsive people, including the spiritual dimension, where she found much of her help. In the end, however, we are responsible to make sure we get the help we need. "It takes time, effort, and faith to mature out of an addictive disposition.... Therapy or no, the ultimate responsibility is still our own" (*Love and Addiction*, Stanton Peele).

3. **Get a new perspective**. Many people, both Cleanies and Messies, find that a spiritual dimension in their lives helps moderate their extremes. A good friend of mine, a compulsive Cleanie, noticed that she became less compulsive about neatness as she matured as a believer. The fruit of the Spirit, says the apostle Paul, is temperance. Temperance is moderation in action, thought, or feeling. Those who have God's Spirit have His help in modifying the drive to save, leave things out, and overcrowd the calendar. A

personal relationship with God also gives us a sense of who we are and why we were created. Knowing our intrinsic value tempers our compulsion to prove who we are through extreme behavior.

4. Begin new behavior. The new behavior will not be as comforting as the old, nor as self-destructive. In *Hope: New Choices and Recovery Strategies for Adult Children of Alcoholics*, Emily Marlin writes, "It is important to note that it's not unusual to feel a sense of loss after giving up an addiction—even when abstinence is desperately wanted." She speaks of addiction in terms of alcohol addiction, but her insights apply to others as well, including messiness. "Giving up the alcohol means the alcoholic also has to give up a certain lifestyle that, though destructive, meets some of his or her needs."

Recovering from messiness is not like overcoming any other problem because messiness involves so much of what we must do every day. When arising, the Messie must make the bed, not walk away from it as before. After breakfast, she must clear the table and take care of the dishes, not pile them on the counter. When the mail comes, she has to handle it immediately instead of putting it in a pile. In addition to establishing "doing" habits to replace "neglecting" habits, the recovering Messie is faced with the years of neglect gathered in every corner of the house. When a person gives up smoking or drinking, she is faced with *stopping* and staying stopped. When a person gives up messiness, she is faced with *starting* and continuing a number of things.

Recovering from messiness is also different from smoking and drinking in that it requires moderation, not abstinence. Moderation is hard for compulsive people. Abstinence is easier. A reforming Messie must decide what to keep and what to get rid of. She can't get rid of everything. Recovering from messiness may be compared to recovering from overeating. A person must eat something. The trick is to do it moderately.

Life is a marathon, not a sprint.

On the whole, Messies are not naturally moderate. They overdo in what they keep and they overdo in their activities. One of the problems a recovering Messie will face is the desire to overdo in the other direction and want to get the house under too much control. Messies who catch the vision of the new way of life want it right away. More than one Messie has exhausted herself by plunging headlong into changing the house. With a jaded eye she looks back over her short experience of trying to change and assures herself that she has proved that it does not work. She can never change. She tried and failed. What she did was exchange one compulsion for another. No wonder it didn't work. A moderate, sustained approach works best. As I frequently remind Messies, life is a marathon, not a sprint. A person may slip and return to her old habits. Studies have shown that this does not mean that all is lost. When she returns to the recovery program she is stronger than when she first started and can continue with hope for success.

Much is being written about compulsive behavior. We are learning more and more. Help is available from many sources. The compulsion to messiness is an area in which much work needs to be done. We do not need to wait for the final results before we get help for ourselves, however. Many people have overcome messiness already. If more powerful techniques arise, wonderful. But in the meantime we can be free.

Assess the Mess

1. Which of the five signs of obsessive-compulsive behavior in Dr. Milkman's checklist do you have?

   a.

   b.

   c.

2. If you recognize compulsive behavior in yourself and think you might profit from outside help, what steps will you take?

   a. Start or join a Messies Anonymous self-help group, an adult children of alcoholics group, or a mental health group that deals with compulsions.

   b. Start therapy with a professional skilled in treating compulsions. If you choose this option, look for a psychiatrist (or someone associated with a psychiatrist) so that medication, if necessary, can be prescribed.

3. Do you notice any compulsive tendencies in any areas other than housekeeping (eating, gambling, drinking, relationships, etc.)? Explain.

7

PARENTING

THE CHILD WITHIN

ANN LOVED HER FATHER. No one treated her any better than he did—when he was sober. But as Ann grew older, her father's sober times grew shorter. By the time she entered high school her father's job got all his sober moments. For a long time Ann believed that if she could be a better daughter her dad would come home instead of getting drunk. Her efforts to please him by being neat led Ann to borderline compulsive behavior. Whatever she did, she did perfectly. She didn't just clean closets; she arranged them like a display window. Soon Ann got to the point that she didn't have time to put anything where it belonged because it took too long to arrange it perfectly. As a result, her bedroom became piled with clothes, shoes, and accessories that she didn't put away because doing so would destroy the order in her closet. Ann's efforts to control her father by controlling her own behavior caused her to lose control of everything. She became a slave to her own unrealistic demands.

The chapter on addiction mentions that adult children of alcoholics are at maximum risk of developing addictive behavior. It may be true, therefore, that people who are powerless to organize their lives were raised in homes made dysfunctional by alcoholism, divorce, mental illness, depression, violence, or abuse.

This chapter shows how people learn to relate to disorganization in childhood. It will be of special interest to those who know, or vaguely suspect, that the homes in which they were raised were dysfunctional.

Messies frequently mention to me that they are members of a self-help group other than Messies Anonymous. They usually belong to a twelve-step group such as Alcoholics Anonymous, Overeaters Anonymous, or Al-Anon. As mentioned in the chapter on addiction, it is not unusual for people to be dealing with more than one problem area at a time, since addictions and compulsions commonly travel in groups.

If a dysfunctional childhood is at the core of your disorganization, success in changing will come about only by facing and resolving those core issues. One of the first things we need to do is to clean out the old ways of thinking and feeling that cause us to act in such self-destructive ways. We need to make space for new thinking, which will lead us to the order, beauty, and peace we seek.

In the early 1980s a group of people who had been raised in dysfunctional families, usually alcoholic families, banded together under the auspices of Al-Anon Family Groups to help each other overcome the negative effects of their childhood experiences. Since that time, the group, called Adult Children of Alcoholics (ACOA), has grown phenomenally, attesting to the need many people have for help.

Some of the general characteristics of adult children of alcoholics correspond with a Messie's struggles in adult life.

1. **Control.** In *Guide to Recovery: A Book for Adult Children of Alcoholics*, Gravitz and Bowden state that control is the one word that most characterizes the interactions of adult children of alcoholics. The authors apply it to interpersonal relationships, but it also applies to housekeeping. Paradoxically, a messy house is frequently the result of a Messie's effort to stay in control of her life. She has gathered and stored more than necessary so she will always have what she needs. Much of it is sitting out for easy access.

One reason that "how to" approaches to cleaning do not work for many people is that they do not address the fear of being out of control. Emily Marlin speaks of this fear in her book *Hope: New Choices and Recovery Strategies for Adult Children of Alcoholics*: "The conflict, confusion, and chaos in the alcoholic home made it seem necessary for us to try to exert control over ourselves and others, simply in order to survive. We had to stay in control in spite of, and because of, the terrible fear that any minute everything could spin out of control."

Many people do not realize that hoarding things and keeping them in view is an attempt at control.

A child whose needs have been chronically ignored because of the family's primary obligation to alcohol learns to subjugate and minimize her own needs.

---

2. **Over-responsible and Under-responsible.** When the adults in a family are dysfunctional, a child will often step in to meet the needs of the family. She tries to carry the load that the adults in the family have dropped. Sometimes this works, and the child, by becoming an "adult," is able to meet with some success in helping the family, albeit at the expense of her own childhood. I believe this is one reason many Messies feel responsible to be the "mother of the world." As children, they put aside their own needs to meet the needs of others. As adults, that is all they know how to do. Many sincere and responsible adults continue in this destructive role forced on them in childhood.

This mother-of-the-world feeling is one reason ACOA Messies cram their lives so full of altruistic activities, such as Boy Scouts, church work, jobs in the healing or helping professions, commitment to causes and charities. These are worthy activities when balanced with other aspects of life. But the person who reacts in a mechanical way to meeting needs goes to an extreme that is self-destructive.

In another way, however, ACOA Messies may be under-responsible. Years of struggling against a power larger than themselves, and losing, has taught them that some things are beyond their control. They feel defeated. Disorderliness, for many, is one of the overwhelming forces they feel unable to control. Claudia Black, in her bestselling book *It Will Never Happen to Me*, states that adult children of alcoholics "feel no sense of power of choice in the way they live." She does not apply this powerlessness to environment, but I believe that some ACOAs act out this approach in the organization of their homes.

There are two other possibilities when considering the ACOA's relationship to disorder. Even though their childhood houses may have been neat, they have lived in personal chaos for so long that they have learned to tolerate a great deal more mess than one would guess possible. Indeed, some may prefer the stimulation of chaos, fearing that life in a neat and orderly house would be boring.

The second thought to consider is that the house is a reflection of the chaos that still exists within the heart of the ACOA. Clutter in the home will not dissipate until the clutter in the heart, which it reflects, is cleaned up.

Many ACOA members are able to control the disorder in their lives. As a matter of fact, extreme neatness is one of the comforts many such children find in a chaotic world. While mom and dad fought and threw things around, their children found comfort in neatly folded underwear and meticulously aligned hangers in the closet. As stated earlier, extreme neatness and extreme messiness are different ends of the same continuum. Some go one way and some go another in response to the stress in their lives.

Writing to me about the help she had found in my previous books, a Messie shared the following thoughts. They illustrate how chaos passes from one generation to another and how one child reacted to that chaos with her own version of control.

As a child, I was often told by my mother that I was a slob. My mother once found termites on the windowsills and launched into a half-hour tirade that it was all because I ate cookies in the living room. "I need order! I hate dirt!" she would often say. What wasn't mentioned was that she was chronically depressed and an alcoholic. This was a result of a horrible childhood, but it was never brought up. Denial and self-delusion lived in our house with us. At the age of sixteen I caught my first glimmer of the real truth. Mom was sleeping, and I went searching the kitchen cabinets for something to eat. We had always had a problem with tiny bugs in our kitchen, but Mom would blame it on the fact that we used oil heat "and everyone knows grease attracts bugs." On the top shelf of the cabinet over the stove was a pile of two-year-old spaghetti boxes, flour bags, sugar bags (none of them sealed), and, of course, lots of happy, busy bugs. It finally dawned on me that I wasn't the only "slob" in the house, and from that time on I put myself in charge of keeping the cabinets in order.

3. **Ignoring their own needs and feelings.** One of the emphases throughout this book is how to tune in to our own needs. This has a much broader application than housekeeping, of course, but our goal is to see how living in a dysfunctional family may create problems in the housekeeping area. We create much of the dysfunctional living in our homes because we do not care enough about our own needs for beauty, our personal tastes, or our need to have the proper equipment. A child whose needs have been chronically ignored because of the family's primary obligation to alcohol learns to subjugate and minimize her own needs.

Alcohol-involved family members may have been doing the best they could to meet the child's needs, but their primary commitment was to the alcohol. This lack of attention eventually leads to the child's low self-esteem, the backbone of addictive and compulsive behavior. The child begins to believe that her needs are not being met because she is not important. Eventually she feels guilty about expressing her own needs because she believes she is imposing on others.

This failure to recognize or express her own needs may lead the Messie to try to do without, to deny herself the things average successful housekeepers take for granted. The ACOA Messie may feel uncomfortable asking her family's help with chores or spending family money on the house. Enough of this self-denial may eventually frustrate the Messie to the point where she explodes, demands help in a tantrum (though she is not quite sure what kind of help she needs), feels guilty about her behavior, and returns to the chronic denial of her needs until the frustration explodes again.

In a similar way, the child in a dysfunctional home learns to subjugate and ignore her own emotions. She is afraid of anger because she remembers the destruction it caused in her home. She was told that nothing was wrong when she knew something was very wrong. She was expected to have patience and understanding far beyond her years, and to control confusion and impatience she learned to suppress her emotions. They just caused trouble. To escape the grim realities of home and to avoid dealing with emotions, she filled her life full of activities. Today she still packs her calendar full, partly out of habit and partly to keep the feelings in abeyance.

This avoidance of emotion carries into her adult life in ways that may not be apparent on the surface. For instance, the Messie who doesn't know what she prefers cannot settle on any particular decorating style. Nothing really excites her. This may be why practicality, not beauty, plays such a strong role in some Messies' thinking. Beauty involves emotions and feeling, practicality doesn't.

When I have a cold I tend to eat more. Because my sense of taste is lessened I keep eating to find something that satisfies me. In a similar way, the inability to feel may be part of what propels Messies to be excessive collectors. They continually hope to find something that will stimulate the feelings they are missing.

The inability to feel may be part of what propels Messies to be excessive collectors. They continually hope to find something that will stimulate the feelings they are missing.

Emily Martin quotes a list of twenty ACOA characteristics formulated by Thomas Perrin and some of his associates. Four of them bear directly on the problems we have been discussing.

- I have difficulty following projects through to the end.
- I am either super-responsible or super-irresponsible.
- I look for immediate as opposed to deferred gratification.
- I manage my time poorly and do not set my priorities in a way that works well for me.

You may want to know which of the many causes of messiness I have suggested is the real one. Is it A.D.D.? Is it compulsive behavior? Is it being brought up in a dysfunctional home? The truth is, these things tend to run together. One or all may contribute to the problem of messiness. It is unlikely that all of the factors mentioned apply to you. And some things significant to you may not be covered. The ones I have given are a starting point to examine your own situation and decide how to get help for yourself. In the end, you have the final responsibility for your own recovery.

"It is the spirit in a man, the breath of the Almighty, that makes him understand" (Job 32:8). Having been enlightened, you are now the parent who must raise the confused child within you who is trying to live an adult life without the necessary tools. Go gently. Be kind to yourself. Be as wise as possible. And God bless you.

Assess the Mess

1. Was there a dysfunction in the home you grew up in that may be affecting your life today? What dysfunction? Explain.

2. Does your messiness give you a feeling of control? If so, how?

3. Do you relate to your housekeeping in an overly responsible way? Are you perfectionistic in some aspects of housekeeping? Explain.

4. How do you feel about being irresponsible? Do you relate it to a feeling of powerlessness learned in childhood?

5. What steps will you take to resolve those issues? You may want to read books about growing up in a dysfunctional home. Two of the three mentioned in this chapter have recommended reading lists, and one refers you to various self-help organizations, such as ACOA. For more information about ACOA call your local chapter of Al-Anon (you'll find the number in your phone directory) or call the ACOA headquarters: 800-245-4656. If you are calling from New York the number is 212-302-7240. You may wish to join an existing Messies Anonymous group or start one in your area. For more information see Appendix B.

8

CLEANLINESS & GODLINESS

The Truth of the Matter

IS MESSINESS A MATTER OF MORALITY? Do good and righteous women keep neat houses while lazy and slovenly women live in clutter? Does God exhort those who falter in this area of life to do better?

The Bible is full of vigorous women doing many interesting things. We wonder how they could live the active lives they did and keep up their houses.

Anna, an eighty-four-year-old widow, lived at the temple, where she praised God and waited for the Messiah. Did she leave her little room as neat as a pin each morning when she went to pray? Or was her mind on heavenly matters and her room in a shambles?

What about the working woman? Deborah was a judge who held court regularly long before she went with Barak to war. What kind of house did she keep? Did her husband, Lappidoth, complain that she was spending too much time away and letting things slip at home? Or did he marvel that she was able to keep up so well with all she had to do? Did she have servants? Or did he help?

Lydia, the first European convert, was a businesswoman who sold expensive fabric. Shiphrah and Puah were full-time midwives. It seems that they trained other midwives and directed them as well. Now that is a hectic schedule! Were they able to keep their homes in order?

There is also the remarkable woman of Proverbs 31. She was busy sewing, cooking, buying land, selling it for a profit, and reinvesting in farmland. In addition she was in the wholesale garment business making linen clothing and accessories for retail merchants. This woman was an organizer of herself and others as well.

The Bible shows us women involved in the community, such as those just mentioned. On the whole, however, it shows women involved in activities related directly and specifically to women:

Giving birth, as seen in the lives of Jesus' and Moses' mothers, who both gave birth under very stressful circumstances.

Feeding their families, as seen in the poor widow who tried to feed her sons with only a little oil and meal.

Entertaining, as seen in Sarah when she entertained the angels and in Mary and Martha when they entertained Jesus and His followers.

Caring for sick children, as seen in the Shunnamite woman when her child was taken ill in the field.

Fighting illnesses of their own, as seen in the woman with the issue of blood.

Fighting grief and loss, as seen in the widow whose son died and in Mary and Martha when their brother died.

Using sex to get their way, as did Delilah with Samson.

The Bible is like a Shakespearean play, full of energetic people deeply involved in the stuff of life. Heavenly principles apply very directly to the real events of life. But not a word is spoken about housekeeping.

The Bible covers a long period and encompasses many life-styles. Abraham and his family were nomads living in tents. Excavations from the area of Ur, where he lived before he began his nomadic life, indicate that the civilization was a gracious one. The clothing was beautiful and the jewelry elegant. The women wore elaborate makeup. Some green eye shadow was found still intact in one of the queen's golden pots.

---

*Like a river, things flow into our houses,
and like a dam, we try to conserve
as much of it as we can.*

They lived in a labor-rich society. They had lots of help. The woman of Proverbs 31 speaks of the maidens she had to help her. They did not have many goods to take care of, however. It was not easy to produce items for the house or personal use. Because they traveled frequently and lived in tents, they didn't keep junk. Besides, they did not have malls, mail order catalogs, and credit cards, which make accumulation easy. Like a river, things flow into our houses, and like a dam, we try to conserve as much of it as we can. In those days one piece of clothing was considered a treasure. The use of clothing in bartering is mentioned often. One of the Israelites stole some clothing from Jericho and buried it under his tent. Samson bet several suits of clothing in an unfortunate wager with his wife's friends. The Roman soldiers gambled to see who would win Jesus' cloak, which was special because it had no seam. They were labor rich and product poor.

Our society is the opposite. We do not have much help for the work we have to do, but we have many things to care for. We are product rich and labor poor.

As the Jews later settled into their land and life became more stable, they began to acquire more goods to take care of. Toward the end of the Old Testament, some even had both winter and summer houses. Even so, compared with our affluence, they led simple lives.

From the Bible we get clues about the way people lived in the days of Jesus.

For example, Jesus told the story of the woman who lost a coin and swept the room until she found it. This is one of the few stories in the Bible that even remotely refers to housework.

Mary and Martha provide us some insight into entertainment when Martha complains to Jesus that Mary is not helping her prepare the meal.

Aside from a few incidental bits of cultural information (e.g., they used their roofs for gathering places in much the same way we use porches, and they slept in bed with their families around them) the Bible gives us little insight into what God might have to say about the purpose, use, or condition of our homes.

I consider this to be a good thing for Messies who have trouble following anybody's instructions about housekeeping. At least we can be messy without violating any of our scriptural commands. This frees us to tackle the problem directly without any unnecessary recriminations against ourselves that will only make it harder for us to change.

Sometimes women who wish to change look for an outside force to whip them into action. They try to use God. But God is not a whip we can use to force ourselves to clean the house. Cleanliness, though desirable, is not next to godliness.

One woman, when she wants her children to clean their rooms, asks them if they would like to have Jesus as a guest in the room when it is messy. She told me that they get busy and clean it up when she says this.

Somehow this smacks of using God to obtain our own ends, which is backward. God uses us to obtain *His* ends. I realize that this method gets the kids busy in their rooms. But is she teaching them something about God that God does not teach about Himself? Out of respect for Him we should be careful not to use Him for our own purposes, no matter how good our purposes are.

Well-meaning friends sometimes use what they believe is a valid spiritual approach to the problem of poor housekeeping. One Messie who has a harried schedule, four young children, and a Messie husband, mentioned to her Cleanie friend at church how much she wished for more time to work in her house.

"Well, maybe if you put the Lord first everything would fall into place," the Cleanie friend hesitantly suggested.

"The Lord blesses my house, but He doesn't do the dishes," the Messie responded. "Pardon me if that sounds irreverent, but I know lots of ungodly people with beautiful homes. I have to spend time with the Lord just to survive."

In contrast to this attitude, some Christian women take a particularly nondirective approach to their lives, believing that is the most spiritual. They awaken each day with an attitude of openness to what the day may bring from the Lord. They do not plan their own schedules or make any decision about how to handle their problems. Instead, they rely on God to solve them. Sometimes they say they are praying and waiting on God's direction.

When God created Adam and Eve, He told them to take control of the world around them. He specifically said, "... Have dominion over the fish of the sea, and over the birds of the air ... and over every creeping thing that creeps upon the earth" (Genesis 1:26). A synonym for "dominion" is "control." Men and women were created to take control of the world around them. Some people, however, especially Messies, have such a hard time making decisions that they choose this "spiritual" approach of waiting for God to decide for them. This seems to relieve them of responsibility and adds an aura of holiness. If you are waiting for God's direction, He may be directing you to take control of your life. This does not mean that you take your life out of God's control; it means that you take responsibility for yourself.

When the Bible does not speak directly to a subject we can draw some inferences from God's whispers in creation. God looked at the work He had done and said it was good. Because we are made in God's image, we desperately want to look at our own creation and say that it is good. Disappointment in that area upsets and saddens us. We can't let messiness take over and be happy about it. It is against our natures.

God also whispered to us about the importance of relationships when He said, "It is not good for man to be alone." Messiness is not conducive to building or maintaining important family relationships.

Messiness interferes with our relationship with ourselves. When the house is messy and our lives are disorganized, we lose touch with what is peaceful and noble in ourselves, and our self-image suffers.

Because we are made in God's image
we desperately want to look at our own creation
and say that it is good.

Messiness interferes with our relationships with others. We cannot invite people to our houses and share the good things of God with them. Our children are embarrassed to invite their friends in. We don't even want the repairman to come into certain parts of our house.

Messiness interferes with our relationships with those we love. Instinctively we know that beauty and order are essential to romance. Romance cannot root in clutter. Young men and women go out of their way to look good to each other and to show a tidy, attractive home to those they are interested in. As a teenager, Mary Lou would rather have died than have Johnny drop in when the house was a mess. Without anyone telling her, she knew that clutter puts a damper on romance.

Once married, however, in the heat of living, Mary Lou forgot that. Imperceptibly, romance suffered. Johnny loves her. Their mutual interests provide them with pleasure; their mutual commitment maintains stability in their home. Romance may even grow. But it will never bloom as beautifully as it would in a relaxing and organized environment. It is a tribute to them that they do as well as they do in this hostile environment.

Messiness interferes with our relationship with God. Worship is the expression of a loving relationship with God, and it works in a way similar to romance. Adoration and praise flow much more freely and vigorously in a sunny room with shiny tables and an uncluttered rug. But Mary Lou tries to praise and adore God in a room with unfolded clothes, shoes lying about, and piles of paper

on the table awaiting attention. She says to herself that she does not have any more time for God. It is not just a matter of time. The whole house is discouraging. Mary turns away from God and turns on the television, where everybody has a great-looking house.

It is true that the Bible does not directly say, "Thou shalt not keep a messy house." But it is easy to see that housekeeping has an important place in our personal, family, and spiritual relationships. To develop those relationships to their fullest, we need to respect the need for beauty and order in the house. Messiness is not a moral issue. It is, however, an important personal issue. As in all important issues, God cares and is interested in helping us in our time of need.

Assess *the* Mess

1. If you have trouble keeping your house orderly, do you sometimes think your messiness adversely affects your relationship with God? Do you think these feelings are valid? Explain.

2. A woman in Chicago never got her work done on time because she believed it was her spiritual duty to do everything perfectly because the Bible says, "Be ye perfect." How does the spiritual dimension in your life relate to any compulsive behavior you may have?

3. Do you use your relationship to God to modify or intensify compulsive tendencies? Explain.

4. Can you think of anything not mentioned in this chapter that the Bible says about housekeeping?

5. How does the condition of your house interfere with your relationships with others, such as family, friends, and neighbors?

6. Describe the kind of place you would like to have in your home to meet with God in a worship experience.

9

TO CHANGE

OR NOT TO CHANGE

I HAVE NEVER DONE THAT THING that I wanted to in all my life," said the character Babbitt in the last line of Sinclair Lewis's novel by the same name.

Messies have a tendency to live like Babbitt. They deny themselves as a matter of principle. Many Messies have denied their feelings so long that they are out of touch with themselves and their desires; they don't know their own tastes or what styles or colors they like. They think they need an interior decorator, but what would they tell her? It is hard for Messies to know what to buy to improve the house. They are so used to ignoring themselves that they are unaware of what they are getting along without.

This willingness to live with unmet needs may stem from a background in which a child's needs were chronically ignored. Concerning children from dysfunctional backgrounds, Gravitz and Bowden write, "These are children who will go along with any and every suggestion because they seem unwilling or incapable of making decisions. They will shrug their shoulders and say, 'It doesn't matter,' since they have no sense of their own needs. Somewhere along the line they lose that sense of power and self through a belief that they cannot affect their environment or their own lives." Later the same authors write, "Adult children may find that acknowledging their personal needs leads them to feel guilty, because they have learned to regard their needs as an imposition on others."

One woman I met at a seminar had books lining the floor of her home and did not realize she needed a bookcase. When I suggested she get one she looked surprised. This lack of awareness of our own needs is one reason organizational methods only work partially. They tell you what you *ought* to do but they don't tune you in to what you *want* and *need* to do. If you are struggling with chronic messiness, you are denying yourself without even realizing it.

Learning to keep house is like learning to dance. If there is no feeling for the music, there is only mechanical movement. That's the way it is with housekeeping. Your desires are the music and your housekeeping moves in harmony with it. *Then and only then* will housekeeping become more than a mechanical chore. No joy, no grace, just drudgery.

In medieval times dancing was a symbol for living. God was called the Lord of the Dance.

"I'll lead you on wherever you may be,
I'll lead you on in the dance said he."

Many Messies distrust their own feelings. They fear that if they begin to think in terms of their own tastes, desires, and needs they will become selfish and deny their higher spiritual commitments. It doesn't work that way. Denying one's feelings and tastes is what causes an unbalanced life. When we use the denial approach we are hooked on getting more stuff, finding security in our possessions, and filling our lives so full they can never be fulfilled. Being out of touch with our feelings and needs is why we have all this trouble with our houses. Once we accept our wants and needs, the house comes into balance.

Learning to keep house is like learning to dance.
If there is no feeling for the music,
there is only mechanical movement.

We are nearing the moment of decision when you will have to choose between changing and not changing, between order and disorder, between beauty and chaos. To prepare for that decision you must get in touch with your own desires. Which of these life-styles do you want? Consider the following reasons for getting your house under control and check the ones that express your desires.

Reasons to Get the House Under Control

☐ 1. **So the house will look better for company.** It is embarrassing for people to come over with the house in a mess. When you work like crazy to hide the disorder, you have to keep some messy parts off-limits. You fear they will go into a messy part. That fearfulness takes the joy out of having visitors. You also want to be able to call a repairman and not be embarrassed to let him in. He's not company, but still....

☐ 2. **So the house will look nice for you.** You are tired of living in all this clutter and ugliness. It wears you out to see it all the time.

Although you have gotten used to it to some extent and you try to accept it, living like this takes a lot out of life.

☐ 3. **So the house will work better.** When you can't find things, when you have to move one thing to put another down, when you don't have enough supplies for what you want to do, the house is not working right. You want a cooperative house.

☐ 4. **For a special friend.** You want to have your boyfriend over but you don't want him to see how you live. You want to believe that if he really cares for you he won't care how the house looks, but you know that's not true. How the house looks reflects on you personally, even if you don't think it should.

Messies live from one crisis to another....
Crisis-oriented living keeps you in a constant
state of activity, which makes you feel alive and useful.

☐ 5. **So you can decorate.** You know it is ridiculous to bring lovely things into your house the way it is. Sometimes you try, but it never looks pretty because of the clutter.

☐ 6. **So you can get out without feeling guilty.** For a long time you have had ambivalent feelings about leaving the house. On the one hand you have denied yourself many outings to stay home and "do something about this house." On the other hand, you have looked for opportunities to do things outside the house just to get away from it. You want to get the house in order so you can stay in it happily, or, if you wish, leave without feeling guilty.

☐ 7. **So you won't have to work so hard.** People who don't have messy houses don't seem to work as hard as you do. Doing the simplest job is a big deal in your house. You spend a lot of time looking for things. Just getting dressed can be a chore because you have to locate the clothes in all of the disorganization. You want life to be easier.

☐ 8. **To get others off your back.** Others are constantly nagging about how the house looks. Perhaps your husband has threatened to leave unless you get it cleaned up. Perhaps he has already left.

☐ 9. **Legal reasons.** Some Messies run into legal trouble because of their messiness. Husbands have used their wife's disorganized life-style as a way to gain custody of the children. And sometimes neighbors call, or threaten to call, the zoning, fire, or health departments because they are concerned about the health risk or because they are repulsed by how bad the yard looks.

☐ 10. **Depression.** Life is hardly worth living when you feel as bad as this cluttered house makes you feel. Your self-esteem has hit bottom. You want emotional release from the depression, guilt, and anger you feel.

Reasons to Leave the House Messy

☐ 1. **Lost hope.** The job of changing looks too big. You don't see any hope of success. It is better not to try than to put all that energy and hope into it and fail.

☐ 2. **It takes too much work.** You are the laid-back type. You don't have the attention span or a high enough level of interest to keep the house nice.

☐ **3. Trouble with the family.** You want to change but does your family? They would have a fit if they had to put their things away and keep the house nice.

☐ **4. Destroy your creativity.** You do not want to lose the creativity that is linked to your messiness. You believe messy people are more creative. And more interesting, too!

☐ **5. Other interests.** Keeping the house in order is not one of your priorities. You have other interests, other things, you would rather spend your time and energy on.

☐ **6. Change of self-image.** You think of yourself as messy and disorganized. Who would you be if you changed? Would you suffer some kind of identity crisis?

☐ **7. You don't believe in self-indulgence.** If you start thinking in terms of your own needs and of improving the house so it will be nicer, you might get carried away and become self-centered. You believe it is safer from a spiritual standpoint not to concentrate too much on how the house looks. Other things are more deserving of your time, effort, and interests.

☐ **8. Costs too much.** Getting the house in order would cost too much money, and you have other uses for it. Education, travel, and cultural pursuits matter more. They last forever. Furniture and labor-saving devices are only temporary.

☐ **9. No more excuses.** The house has been your excuse for not doing other things. Once you get the house in order, there will be no end to what you feel obligated to do. You might also feel obligated to invite more people to your house, and you're not sure you want to do that.

☐ **10. You don't deserve a nice house.** Some people are worthy of a nice house, but you think you don't deserve one. So why work at it?

☐ **11. To feel needed.** If the house gets organized you will have nothing else to do, so you will not feel needed.

☐ **12. To exert your authority.** You have a perfect way to exert your will over someone trying to push you around. They want you to clean the house. You don't. So when the house is messy, you win.

☐ 13. **To punish someone.** You use the messy house to get back at somebody. You know you can upset them by keeping a messy house, so you do.

☐ 14. **To test your friendships.** Those who like you in spite of your house are true friends. You can test your friends' sincerity by bringing them into the house. If they like the real you, the house doesn't matter.

☐ 15. **Inability to organize.** Some people have a knack for organizing, but you don't know where to begin or how to continue.

☐ 16. **Fear of making a mistake.** Suppose you throw away something important. Suppose you set up an organizational system that doesn't work. It is better not to make a change than to make mistakes. You don't want to live with regrets.

☐ 17. **Crisis-oriented living.** It is the nature of a Messie to live from one crisis to another. You organize your life to insure that you will always have a crisis of some kind. If none occurs naturally, you will create one. Crisis-oriented living keeps you in a constant state of activity, which makes you feel alive and useful. And all of this activity and chaos keeps you too busy to deal with the more resistant areas of life that you wish to avoid anyway.

Assess the Mess

1. List the reasons you checked for getting your house in order. Add any others you think of. Put a check beside the strongest reasons.

   a.

   b.

   c.

   d.

   e.

2. List the reasons you checked for keeping the house messy. Put a check beside the most significant reasons.

a.

b.

c.

d.

e.

3. When you look at the second list you will see that most of your reasons for keeping your house messy involve fears. Earlier in the book I mentioned that Messies have more emotional involvement with their houses than successful housekeepers have. Messies love their things more intensely. They fear more often and more strongly. It is fear most of all that paralyzes the Messie who devoutly wishes she could change. What fears keep you from getting the house in order?

a.

b.

c.

4. Think of ways to overcome these fears and free yourself to get and keep your house in order. List three steps you might take to overcome the fears that are holding you back.

a.

b.

c.

5. When did you first notice a problem keeping the house in order?

6. How did you first notice it?

7. What happened when you first tried to change?

8. What kept you from success?

9. What has hindered you since that time?

10. Are the reasons the same as the original ones or different?

Leaving the house messy is a viable choice, but it is hard for me to offer it when I know the pain it will bring. While writing this chapter, I spoke to a Messie from Pennsylvania. She has four children; the youngest is seven weeks old. She said she was going to kill herself if she did not get help. Although she said it with a laugh, she wasn't entirely joking. The comment expressed her frustration and impatience with the problem. She is a member of another anonymous group but has not been able to get control of her house by using the group's twelve-step method. She thought she could be successful if she just worked harder and longer, even though her neighbors seemed to be sitting around in their lovely homes not working. To speed herself up to get more done she had taken diet pills. This was not good for her, nor did she feel that it was wise for a mother with young children to take them. She was willing to do almost anything to change. She knew the serenity prayer: "God grant me the ability to accept the things I cannot change, the courage to change the things I can, and the ability to know the difference." Her problem, she said, was that she was unable to change and unwilling to accept herself. "I just can't accept this in myself," she said. The truth was that she was able to accept herself as a Messie (she had been doing it daily, albeit unhappily) and she was also able to change. But she did not know that yet.

You may choose to have a messy house. If you do, you know what ills to expect. If you choose to have an orderly and beautiful house you do not yet know what problems or joys await you. I assure you, however, that you will feel as if a weight has been lifted when your life turns around, not because your house is nice, though that is a very wonderful thing, but because you have a sense of control.

Your choice will also bring new problems. You will make mistakes, but as Walt Whitman said, "The man who can't make a mistake, can't make anything."

According to a fable, a roguish young man heard of a sage who was said to know the hearts of men and could discern things not known to others. To draw attention to his own wisdom, the young man decided to discredit the sage by testing him in such a way that he would have to be wrong. He told his young companions about his plan. He would get a live bird and hold it behind him. He would then ask the sage whether the bird was dead or alive. If the sage said the bird was dead, the young man would show him the bird alive. If the sage said the bird was alive, he would squeeze it to death behind him and show the sage the dead bird.

On the appointed day the young man met the sage with his companions looking on. "Oh great sage," he began, "in my hand I hold a bird. Tell me, is the bird dead or is it alive?"

The sage, who was indeed wise, looked at the young man and at his companions, all waiting for an answer. The young man's scheme was obvious to the sage, so he answered, "The bird is as you will, young man. It is as you will."

You hold the fate of the house in your hands, and the house will be as you will.

Look at the two lists—the reasons to change and the reasons not to change. Which is more powerful in your life? Saying "Yes" to neatness is like saying "I do" in marriage. We know something of the commitment we are making but there are many details we are not aware of. You know what the messy life is like. You do not know what the orderly life is like. You see what it is like for your friends, but you do not know what it will be like for you. As Shakespeare said in *Hamlet*, we often would "rather bear those ills we have than fly to others that we know not of."

It is as you will.

If you have not marked another part of this book, mark this spot. You have four choices.

1. Remain messy and quit fighting it.
2. Remain messy and hate every minute of it.
3. Keep trying harder and working smarter by using new organizational methods to make the house neat.
4. Have an orderly house without struggling with new organizational methods.

The last choice sounds too good to be true, but it is the only one that works. And it works almost like a magic wand because it acts in conjunction with what we really want to do. When we get in touch with that secret, we have a kind of magic. Part 2 of this book tells you how to take hold of your magic wand.

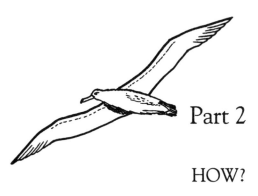

Part 2

HOW?

Overcoming the Messie Mindset

PART 1 DEALT WITH the "Why" of the Messie mindset. This part covers the "How"—how to overcome it. It explores such subjects as why organizational systems don't work, why working harder doesn't work, how to handle the messy family, and how to overcome the stress of living in a disorganized way.

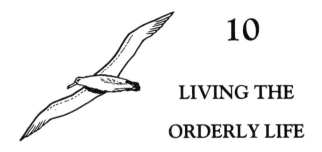

10

LIVING THE

ORDERLY LIFE

A YOUNG MAN from a small midwestern town graduated at the top of his high school class and applied to go to the state university, even though the idea of going to a large school terrified him. Sure, he was a big fish in his small pond, but was he really college material? He filled out the college entrance forms, took the entrance exam, and waited for his scores. The results confirmed his worst fears. Although he had been accepted he was only average in intelligence, perhaps slightly below.

He made miserable grades in his college classes and was about to leave school when his advisor called him in. Why, he wanted to know, was an "A" student suddenly making "D's". The young man explained that his low I.Q. of 98 made it impossible for him to succeed in the classes he was taking. Flabbergasted, the advisor explained that 98 was not his I.Q. but the percentile in which he ranked among all the students who had taken the entrance exam. This information freed the young man. From then on he was back to his all-"A" performance.

As we see from this example, having the ability is not enough. We must also *know* that we have the ability before we will be able to use it. One of the problems of looking closely at our abilities, or lack of them, is that we may get the impression that we are unable to get the house in order.

Even calling ourselves "Messies" may give us the wrong impression of ourselves and make us think we are unable to get the house in order. Nothing could be further from the truth. Getting a house under control requires nothing that we do not have or cannot get. You have an orderly person within you. That is why you are reading this book. You want to let that orderly person out. You need to shift your attention from the messy person's thinking, which has dominated your life, to the orderly person's thinking.

It takes time to make that change. Old thoughts and habits do not melt away overnight. When you approach a closet, drawer, or pile of clothes, do it with detachment. Be good to yourself. Refuse to saddle yourself with all kinds of unnecessary junk because of fear. You know that life is full of things for you; therefore you do not need to grasp every scrap to satisfy yourself.

There are two kinds of thin people: those who are thin and never think about it and those who are thin and are always fighting to stay that way. Many Messies have attained a degree of success in housekeeping, but it is a daily struggle to maintain it because it goes against the grain of what they really want to do. When the struggling Messie begins thinking of housekeeping as her primary desire, her struggling ceases and order emerges. The rest of this book is about getting into that mode of thinking and leaving the old, fearful, unsuccessful one behind.

My own experience with being a Messie has been lengthy. When I first realized what I had been doing to myself I became angry. This anger propelled me into a search for help. The help I found became the basis for my Messies Anonymous program. When I began the program, things started to improve immediately. Order and beauty emerged. Within two weeks, I could see a difference. But basically I was still thinking in the old way while trying to act in a new way. My old way of thinking put obstacles in the way of freedom. However, when I discovered the successful average housekeeper mentality (discussed in chapter 14) things began to change more effortlessly. Old bastions of resistance began to crack and order poured out. The solutions to problems that had remained obscure became clear.

Many Messies who have used the M.A. program successfully will be further helped by this book. Those who haven't used the M.A. approach will find release from the Messie life-style never found by those who changed their housekeeping habits without fully changing their thinking.

Having the ability is not enough.
We must also know that we have the ability
before we will be able to use it.

Be patient with yourself. You are not doing this for your spouse, family, friends, parents, or anybody but yourself. You do not have to prove anything to yourself and certainly not to them. Be prepared to slip. When the change begins, the Messie part of you will see itself shrinking and will try to get you to turn back. It will try to sabotage your success and go back to the more comfortable and familiar Messie life-style. But don't give in.

Many times I was tempted to go back to the old way. The only thing that kept me going was my unwillingness to return to the pain of living that way. My family, whom I had trained to be messy, put up many obstacles. But I, like many others, have found freedom to live in order and beauty.

You do not need discipline or commitment to succeed with this program. All you need is a vision of yourself as a person of worth and dignity living in a way that reflects those qualities. Once this vision is in place, a peculiar thing begins to happen. When all of the forces of sky and earth that have been at work against you see that you will not abandon your dream, they will finally give up and say to each other, "It's not worth it! Let her have her dream!" and they will slink away.

When you let the successful housekeeper out, she will do the job for you. The chapters that follow tell you how to give her freedom.

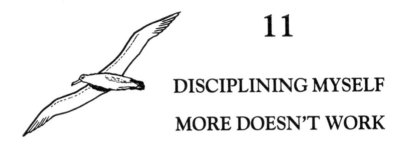

11

DISCIPLINING MYSELF

MORE DOESN'T WORK

HOW MANY PSYCHIATRISTS does it take to change a light bulb?"

"One, but the light bulb has got to *want* to be changed."

This is true of any change we wish to make in our lives. Change comes only when we really want to be changed.

Many Messies are motivated by the idea of a new way of life and will make many changes. They will buy new curtains, get new bookshelves, and give away clutter, but they hold back in challenging a few ways of thinking. The most important change we need to make is in our thinking.

We make the final change when we let go of sacred cow ideas. Until they go, we will contend with the stress of living in two worlds.

You can change, but you must want it.

New beginnings! We love the thought. We want to leave the old problems, the old habits, and in our case, the old clutter, behind. Unfortunately, most of us are not willing to leave behind the most important thing of all—the way we think.

Just as overweight people seek thinness and alcoholics seek sobriety, Messies search for order. Just as smokers look for relief from their habit and gamblers wish to be free of their uncontrollable drive, Messies want to be free of the clutter and disorder that characterize their lives.

Messies are very emotional people. Emotions get them going one day and bring them to a halt the next. Any approach that is going to work for chronically disorganized people is going to have to take emotions into account. This book does.

This high emotional involvement is why Messies do not respond well to pragmatic approaches to orderliness. If they try to use a pragmatic, systematic approach that involves pure willpower to overcome their weaknesses, they may meet with initial success but will probably fall back into the same old patterns of messiness and disorganization. The only thing that will be different will be feelings of increased hopelessness.

Messies are wonderful people. They are enthusiastic, deep, conscientious, full of fun, interesting, interested in many things, and successful in many areas of their lives—but they are failures when it comes to organization.

Because of these common characteristics of Messies, the words *willpower* and *self-discipline* are never heard in the Messies Anonymous vocabulary or used in the M.A. program. Messies do not respond well to approaches based on these concepts. I believe, in fact, that most people do not respond well to these concepts. People talk about discipline as though it is a powerful force in changing behavior. This is mainly talk. Discipline is highly over-rated as a factor in achievement.

We do see discipline at work in the military. Young people who may never have been disciplined in their lives quickly become disciplined under the influence of the boot camp drill sergeant. Things they may never have done and never expected to have to do, they do regularly in the military. They may not want to make their beds or shine their shoes, but they do. That is discipline: Doing what you don't want to do. The reason they do it, of course, is because they don't want to get in trouble. They may be totally undisciplined off the base. And when they go home, they may not make their beds or shine their shoes. But for a short time, with the sergeant's supervision, they are disciplined.

Discipline is highly overrated
as a factor in achievement.

We also see discipline in the lives of artists, both in fine arts and the performing arts. We see it in the lives of athletes. To excel in their fields, artists and athletes put in long hours of hard work, excluding other interests and demands on their time, so they may someday paint a masterpiece, play in Carnegie Hall, or go to the Olympics. Further inspection will show us, however, that this discipline may not be a part of their lives in every aspect. Athletes who discipline themselves for their sport may live a wild and unruly life when practice is over.

When we look at people who exhibit great discipline in their lives, we see that it is generally in one area and sometimes, as in the case of athletes, it is for a short period of time.

But what about everyday discipline? There *are* people who live well-ordered lives. Their checkbooks are always up to date, their houses are tidy, their cars are washed, and their laundry is folded and put away. They seem to do this effortlessly while others (the undisciplined ones, we assume) are running amuck trying to keep their houses within the national allowable range of clutter. Why is this?

Many people think discipline is the result of willpower. They say things like: "I can't lose weight because I don't have enough willpower." "I need more willpower to stop smoking." "I could stop gambling if I had enough willpower." Or, as many of us say, "I just don't have enough willpower to keep up with the house. I need more discipline."

Rather than willpower and discipline,
Messies need focus.

It does not help to quote platitudes such as "Where there is a will there is a way" to the floundering Messie. It does not help to tell her to have a stronger will, to put her nose to the grindstone and her shoulder to the wheel. This just causes confusion and guilt in the person you are trying to encourage. These platitudes may be true, but they are not the answer to the Messie's problem. Telling a Messie these things is like telling a man whose car is immobilized by transmission problems that using high-octane gasoline will make it run better. It may be true that higher octane gas makes cars run more smoothly, but that does not help him because his problem has nothing to do with combustion. Admonishing someone to be more disciplined or have stronger willpower helps only those whose lives are already running pretty well. It does not get to the root of the Messie's problem. She must get something else fixed before she can even begin to consider the place discipline may have in her life.

Rather than willpower and discipline, Messies need focus. Messies are not generally focused on what they want to do in the house. They only want things better in some foggy sense. If you are able to focus on what it is that you want to do for your house, the house will begin to change automatically. The discipline and willpower will come if they are needed.

Focus is an interesting thing. With simple adjustments photographers can change the focus of a picture from the foreground to the background. With the foreground in focus, the background disappears in a blur. Likewise, successful housekeepers who focus clearly on their homes have learned to leave secondary things out of focus.

The problem with Messies is that many things keep their interest in lovely homes out of focus. Practicality, for example, distorts focus. Many practical ideas mess up the house. You may want a stationary bicycle for exercise. Where better to put it than in the living room? Your mother-in-law is giving away some furniture. You take it, even though you don't need it, because you hope someday to move into a larger place where you can use it. In the meantime your family is using small paths to get through the crowded house. You can vegetables but you have no place to store the jars so you stack them on your kitchen counter for the winter. Or perhaps you stack the empty canning jars on the kitchen counter in case you decide to can in the future. All of these practical ideas end up making the house untidy and hard to live in.

The next unfocuser that Messies need to watch out for is any activity that conflicts with the care of a beautiful home. Sometimes these activities seem as though they will add beauty to the home, but they clutter it instead. Crafts, for instance, can undermine beauty. A Messie who wants to beautify her home may take a tole painting or cross stitching class. Many of her friends do it. She can socialize and make something nice for her house. The project may turn out lovely, but few people will appreciate its beauty if the house is a mess because she left her supplies out.

The time and money spent on tole painting or cross stitching would have been better spent on bringing the main part of the house into focus. She has been working hard to improve the house and she wonders why it doesn't look any better than before. She does not realize that her time was misspent because it was unfocused.

Sometimes this lack of focus is at the heart of the interior decorating problem. The Messie woman gathers such a variety of eclectic materials that no style nor color scheme dominate. People say to her, "Your house is so interesting." But no one says her house is lovely. She has all the necessary pieces; they just don't work together. She needs to realize that some wonderful but unmatched things must go if the beautiful and orderly house is to come together. You do not need discipline or willpower to make your life organized and successful. You only need to know how to focus your attention and effort where it will make a difference.

What appears to be willpower is actually want power. People who keep nice houses focus on their desire for a lovely and orderly home. They don't have to strive to get their houses to conform. The houses just do. They do not have a white-hot burning passion for a perfect house. They just have a comfortable warm desire for a nice one. It never occurs to them to settle for less. Why should it? For them it is no struggle to maintain their homes as they want them because they maintain their focus.

As mentioned before, when we bring one part of the picture into focus, it makes other parts fuzzy. When we begin to emphasize the house, other areas of life will get less attention. To focus our attention in productive ways, we must decide which unnecessary things we are doing that focus our attention away from the overall order and beauty of our houses. When we eliminate these, our lives will be disciplined without having to use willpower and without having to keep our noses to the grindstone.

Sometimes we need others to help us focus on what we want and to keep our commitment in focus. Friends, or a group of friends (we call this an M.A. Self-Help Group), can help us verbalize our desires and thereby sharpen our focus. We will have a force even stronger than willpower—a sharply focused "want power."

Assess the Mess

1. Do you suffer from lack of focus as it relates to your house? Explain.

2. One Messie told me that one day when she could no longer stand her messy house she cleaned the ceiling fan first, even though the house was so cluttered she could hardly find a place on the floor for a chair she needed to stand on to do the job. She had the needs of the house out of focus. Describe several incidents that illustrate your lack of focus.

   a.

   b.

   c.

3. Name several things that unfocus your attention (e.g., hobbies, children's activities, volunteer activities, practicality, etc.). Explain briefly. Put a check beside the ones you can give up or do more moderately.

   a.

   b.

   c.

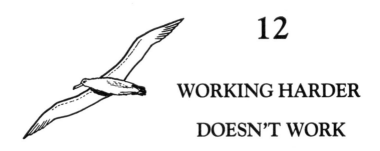

12

WORKING HARDER

DOESN'T WORK

Horatio Alger, Jr., a nineteenth-century American minister and novelist, wrote about 120 books for boys. Most of Alger's characters were poor bootblacks or newsboys whose virtue and hard work were invariably rewarded with riches and success. Some people believe that Alger's books contributed to the American mindset that believes hard work always results in success. Perhaps they also contributed to a similar but more dangerous mindset—that laziness is always the cause of failure.

J. Paul Getty, U.S. oil executive and millionaire, knew that success involves a lot more than just hard work. In response to a request from a magazine for a short article explaining his success, Getty wrote: "Some people find oil. Others don't."

Getty recognized that he had done nothing special to earn his wealth.

In the same way that working harder doesn't always make us rich, it doesn't always make us neat either. But Messies are programmed to think that laziness is to blame for their lack of housekeeping success. They try to think of themselves as imaginative or interesting, but in the back of their minds the word *lazy* keeps echoing.

Occasionally you will see an article about the problem of collecting too much and having clutter all around. Usually these articles are written tongue-in-cheek. The author is trying to show that she is a bit eccentric. But hey! that just makes her all the more lovable, doesn't it? Andy Rooney is one of those people—messy but affable.

Long ago people laughed at drunks. They would imitate their stumbling and show how funny it was that they couldn't get the key in the lock or speak without a slur. Those jokes are no longer fashionable because people see drunkenness for the serious problem that it is. Fat people used to be thought of as jolly. Now we know that many overweight people laugh only to cover their tears. Messiness is still a joke to many people. But it is not funny to the people who have it.

Messies want a life of order and dignity. They don't want to look forever for the flashlight, hammer, or keys. They want to lead comfortable, controlled lives. And so they search for methods to overcome their madness. Some methods don't work at all; others work for a while and then falter. These methods all fall under the category of the *Work Harder Approach*.

The Work Harder Approach acknowledges all kinds of reasons for disorder: the size of the house, the number of people in it, the number of activities, the lack of cooperation from others. But in the end, the responsibility falls on one person. You. And if the house is not in order you believe it is because you have not worked hard enough.

Those who try the Work Harder Approach use willpower, rules, and systematic methods. They believe that if they discover the right method and use it faithfully, their problem will be over. They think something is wrong with them because their house is not under control, and they believe it even more strongly when messiness overcomes them again. They blame themselves, not the method, for their failure.

Some of the premises of the Work Harder Approach are:

1. **Clutter is bad.** They are convinced that cleanliness is next to godliness or some modification of that slogan. Good people are neat. Bad people are slobs.

Messies already work hard enough.
Some Messies work harder than
successful housekeepers.

---

2. **Organization is an endless chore.** Some programs use lists, cards, or a variation of the two. These bring some order out of the chaos, but they also confirm to the Messie what she suspected— housecleaning is a gigantic chore. With an extra large dose of determination she tackles the system, but eventually slips back into the clutter of the old way of life. Now she has to deal not only with the hassle of disorganized living, but with the disappointment of failure. She is now certain that she is at fault.

3. **The cleaning marathon will do the trick.** Sometimes the frustration of living in this yucky house gets to be such a hassle that the Messie goes on a cleaning binge. Everything out! Everything put away! One of the chief problems that Messies have is the urge to do a lot fast. She takes two or three days to clean the house for

company, and for one day the things she stuffed into drawers, closets, and cabinets stay there. On the next day they burst out, and the house returns to its normal state, or worse.

The Messie feels two things—pride that for a moment she had a lovely house, and disappointment that she was not able to maintain it for more than a day.

In *Flowers for Algernon*, a mentally retarded young man is cured of his retardation. But then the treatment begins to wear off and he returns to his retarded condition. We grieve with him as he sees himself faltering. We leave the theatre sad. Messies live that play again and again as they try to function normally, only to fall back into their old ways. The cleaning marathon just leads to more failure.

4. Self-denial is a part of good housekeeping. Subconsciously Messies believe that to have a clean house they will have to give up the things they love to do. They are convinced that there is not time enough to do the fun things, or the important things, and to have a clean house as well. Most Messies aren't willing to sacrifice their way of life for neatness.

But self-denial, in its own way, is also a part of the Messie life-style, though few realize it. Messies already deny themselves every day. They deny themselves the pleasure of inviting people to their house because they are embarrassed by the mess. They also deny themselves the food they like to eat because they never have the necessary ingredients to make it. And some even deny themselves the pleasures of outside activities because they feel guilty leaving the house in such terrible condition.

5. Working harder will bring about the change you want. The trouble with this approach is that working harder will never bring to light the reasons you are messy. Messies already work hard enough. Some work harder than successful housekeepers. Until we uncover the underlying causes of messiness, the house will never change.

Clarence Darrow, a renowned U.S. lawyer, recognized early that hard work wasn't the only road to success. Darrow was being interviewed for a magazine article on the reasons given by prominent men for their success. "Most of the men I've spoken to so far attribute their success to hard work," said the interviewer.

"I guess that applies to me, too," said Darrow. "I was brought up on a farm. One very hot day I was distributing and packing down the hay which a stacker was constantly dumping on top of me. By noon I was completely exhausted. That afternoon I left the farm, never to return, and I haven't done a day of hard work since."

Assess the Mess

Messies are perfectionists who frequently make a big deal out of everything and want to get every answer exactly right. But for these exercises, don't be particular. The first impulse will be the best. Write down what comes to your mind first.

1. When you have tried to get the house in order in the past, what has happened?

2. What approaches have you used in the past and how well have they worked?

3. Look at the characteristics of the Work Harder Approach. Which ones involve you? Describe your experiences.

   a.

   b.

   c.

13

ARRESTING

MESS STRESS

Sᴛʀᴇss ᴀɴᴅ ᴅɪsᴏʀɢᴀɴɪᴢᴀᴛɪᴏɴ go hand in glove, so Messies have more stress than most people. A cluttered life is a stress-filled life.

I am not just talking about frayed nerves but actual wear and tear on the body as it attempts to adjust to change. These changes may be good, like getting married, or bad, like getting a divorce, but both create stress. These stressors may be physical or mental, but they all affect the body. And if they happen regularly, or if several happen in a short enough time, they eventually affect how we live and keep our houses.

The American College of Physicians has put together the following checklist of symptoms that indicate a person may be under stress and should see a doctor for advice.

- Heart palpitations, chest pains, tightness in the chest.
- Fear of leaving the house.
- Insomnia or excessive sleeping.
- Loss of interest in usual activities.
- Fatigue, headaches, or other physical symptoms.
- Sadness or morbid thoughts.
- Worsening of existing illness without a clear explanation.

These, of course, are medical symptoms that may be caused by something other than stress.

Other sub-clinical symptoms may be signs of stress.

- Increased forgetfulness (locking yourself out of the car, forgetting appointments or mixing them up, increased messiness). Stress tends to accentuate whatever weaknesses we already have. That is why Messies tend to become more disorganized, forgetful, distractible, and messy under stress. A Cleanie becomes more fanatically neat under stress.
- Anthropomorphizing inanimate objects. Belongings take on a life of their own. You feel that you must protect them and that they are out of your control. They go (get lost) and come (get found) on their own.
- Repeated colds, flu, etc. Stress weakens our resistance to disease.
- Skin problems.
- Being easily upset by unpleasant things that happen.

These are symptoms that doctors and psychologists describe and analyze. We may recognize stress as the point where we feel tired of people asking too much of us, tired of us asking too much of ourselves, tired of working too hard, tired of not being appreciated. In short, we are just plain tired.

Two kinds of women experience the most stress. One is the controller. She is under stress because neither people nor things will cooperate completely. Controllers control for a couple of reasons. First, they are afraid of things that are out of control. Second, they simply like the power of being in control.

Messies are not generally controllers, but they relate to their messiness in a controlling way. No one is allowed to touch their things or to make any changes in the house that will involve their things. Woe to the reforming Messie wife who has to tackle a controlling Messie husband as well as the messy house.

The other type of woman under stress is the pleaser. Pleasers want life to go well for everybody. That is one reason they keep so many things. It is not only so that they will be well supplied; they want to have whatever anyone else will ever need as well.

Many of these people use their many skills to please others in their jobs and often become very successful. The truth is, however, that although they are capable, friendly, and highly thought of, they have very low self-esteem. That's why they try so hard to please everyone. If they are going to be successful at this impossible task, they must not make any mistakes. To make sure everyone likes them, they say "yes" to every job they are asked to do. They carry more of the load in the family than anyone. They may even go out searching for more activities to confirm their abilities.

In short, to keep up their image of being perfect and to avoid criticism (to which they are very sensitive) pleasers abandon control of their lives and priorities for the sake of others. Since pleaser women often marry controller men, their lives are frequently overstocked with jobs and responsibilities given to them by their husbands. Although they may complain about being taken advantage of, they are committed to this self-destructive way of life.

Studies indicate that the feeling of helplessness in controlling one's life is a major source of stress. If a dog in your neighborhood is barking loudly, you may become nervous and feel jumpy. If you are trying to sleep, each bark is like a hammer in your head. You wonder why the owners don't make the dog stop barking. If you are the owner, however, the dog's barking may not disturb you nearly as much. Why not? Because you are in control. You know that you can call the dog in and get relief from the noise. Because you know you have the power to change the annoyance, it doesn't bother you nearly as much.

You may have noticed the same phenomenon in restaurants or church when young children make disturbing noises. The parents sit blithely by, seemingly oblivious to the racket. Yes, they are used to the noise of their own children and therefore not as easily distracted by it. But they also know they have some control over the situation, and this relieves their stress about it.

The Result of Stress

In addition to the results we notice—chest pains, forgetfulness, and fatigue—stress causes many results that can go unnoticed for a long time.

What you don't see going on in your body is your tense muscles, furrowed brow, clenched jaw, and racing heart. Your body shuts down water flow, causing dryness in the mouth. Blood flow is restricted. Adrenaline pours into the system and other glands react to it. Externally, we are going about our business. Internally, our bodies are fighting to keep things on an even keel. We become so used to it we think our bodies feel that way naturally. Nothing could be further from the truth.

Help for the Stressed-out Messie

Help comes in two packages. One is called cure and the other prevention.

The Cure

1. Exercise is the greatest stress reliever. Such activities as walking, biking, and yoga get the blood flowing and the body moving to ease out the knots of stress. When the heart starts to pump and the lungs start to pull in good clean air, the mind begins to see things more clearly. Life looks better. Sleep comes easier as well.

Tension usually affects the head and neck, so the following exercises focus on those areas. And most of them are stretching exercises, since muscles begin to shorten as they are tensed by stress. You can do them while sitting down. Most of them can be done in public places without fear of looking weird. Some you can do in your car, but home is always a good place.

a. The Neck Roll. Bend your head forward as though nibbling the button off your blouse. Then roll your head over to your shoulder, forward again, to the other shoulder, and back to the front. Repeat several times. (A more familiar version of this exercise has you roll your head toward your back, but recent medical studies have shown that this is unhealthy.)

The feeling of helplessness
in controlling one's life
is a major source of stress.

---

b. The Shoulder Shrug. Hunch your shoulders up as high as you can toward your ears, as though you were indicating, "I don't know." Rotate them forward, down, back, and up again. Do this two or three times in both directions.

c. The Big Hug. Hold your arms out to the sides parallel to the floor. Keeping them as high as possible while standing straight, touch your hands together behind you. Now bring them forward across your body to your shoulders and give yourself a big hug. Even if the stretch doesn't work wonders, the hug will.

d. The Stretch. Lift your hands high over your head as though reaching for something. Keep them there for a few seconds. Lower them. Then do the same with one hand at a time. Do this until you feel relief in the back and shoulders.

e. Massage. Take time to gently massage your neck and shoulders, rubbing in circles on those tight muscles until they begin to soften a little.

2. Relax in a warm tub filled with bubble bath. Soaking in a candlelit bathroom can do wonders. A friend with whom I shared

this idea said she is going broke buying candles and bubble bath because she likes it so much.

3. A massage and hot tub. If they're available, this combination can also do the trick, but most of us will have to settle for a simple bubble bath.

Prevention

I saw a bumper sticker that said "I *Can* Have It All." I should have looked to see if the driver was a frazzled wreck. If she wasn't, she was probably at the beginning stage of having it all. People at that point are still full of energy and excitement. Life is full of wonderful things to do and be and have. Messies, being wonderful people who appreciate the good, creative things in life, don't want to miss any. We get high on having it all. When it's out there, it's hard not to go for it.

At the middle stage of having it all some stress begins to show. But the excited "haver" still believes that if she just organizes things a little tighter, she can fit them all in. Her time for herself is the first thing to go, of course. But no matter. These other things are all so much more important.

At the final stage of having it all, things begin to get out of control. One meeting cancels another. An obligation makes it impossible to go to the children's program. Nothing seems important anymore. Cooking has been greatly curtailed so she can meet her obligations. She videotaped some television programs she really wanted to see, but she has no time to watch them. They are just another pressure.

A woman in the final stages might not look frazzled because she is trying to keep up a good face. Many people would say she is successful. She hardly recognizes that she is not. She looks okay on the surface but inside she is ragged. She will eventually feel the effects of the stress she has put herself under because she did not know the one secret of avoiding stress. Instead of trying to have it all she should have been learning to set priorities, the secret of stress prevention.

For Messies, this is hard to accept. They want to avoid the decisions necessary for setting priorities. And they don't like saying no to a worthy cause. They recognize the needs of the world and want to help. And some of their activities bring in extra money. They wouldn't want to have to give that up. In short, Messies want to believe the "I *Can* Have It All" bumper sticker, but it's a lie.

Nobody can have it all. We must set priorities according to what is important and not be lured from our commitment. Picture the bumper sticker that says "I *Can* Have It All." Paste over it another sticker, one that says *Priorities*.

To make the change, we must replace our old way of thinking. It is not easy cutting back on the hectic life. We have grown accustomed to the excitement and may even be hooked on the adrenaline surge we get from it. Although the price we must pay for this new way of thinking seems high, the results are worth it. Here's how it's done.

1. **Lead an evenly paced life**. Find your best rhythm and stick to it. I am an early morning person. I go to bed about nine o'clock every night and wake up about quarter after five every morning. I don't deviate very much from this routine. Sometimes I must stay up later. On a really wild night I may go entirely berserk and stay up as late as eleven. But I pay for it the next day, and as soon as possible I get back into my routine.

In *Body Rhythm: The Circadian Rhythms Within You*, author Lee Weston tells of studies showing that if we get too far out of our natural circadian rhythm we bring stress into our lives, resulting in physical problems. People who lead stressful lives can't deviate as much from their regular schedule as those who live less pressured lives.

Everyone's rhythm cycle is different. But if you find yours and stick to it, you will be stronger than if you're always wasting energy fighting your own body.

2. **Make time for things that bring emotional support**. It may be a church group. Dr. Gene Stainbrook, quoted in *Unstress Your Life: How to Reduce Tension and Feel Great* by the editors of *Prevention* magazine, says that church involvement gives people many supports that help alleviate stress.

Another help may be a Messies Anonymous support group. *Health* magazine makes the following observation on the place of self-help groups in reducing stress:

In a large midwestern city, three men and two women meet for dinner every Tuesday. No matter how delicious the food, by mid-meal they have clearly forgotten everything but the intense, low-voiced conversation they are conducting. No, they're not gossip columnists exchanging the latest dirt—they're ordinary people talking out their tensions in one of the informal self-help groups now springing up all over the country. No one in the group is a professional therapist, but the support they give each other is so valuable that the group has met steadily for a year (March, 1984).

One of the most encouraging things I do for myself is listen to the radio on my way to work. In our area we have four inspiring stations. Two are religious stations that play glorious hymns. Frequently I arrive at work at 7:30 in the morning having sung the great hymns of faith heartily all the way to work. I am one of the few people who comes to work whistling and humming. I find it a wonderful way to start the day. Sometimes I listen to soaring classical music. At other times I listen to a station that plays tapes of great motivational speakers such as Zig Ziglar, Famous Amos The Cookie Man, and Wayne Dyer.

Whatever things are true, whatever things are noble, whatever things are just, whatever things are pure, whatever things are lovely ... meditate on these things.

(Philippians 4:8 NKJV)

What inspires me may not inspire you. Search your soul to find out what encourages you. For instance, if great literature thrills you, you may wish to go back to college and study it.

3. **Replace negative thoughts with positive ones.** Don't dwell on bad news in the paper. Don't ponder problems on the television news. Avoid people who are fascinated by bad news and negative thoughts. We are the first people in history to know within minutes about a tragedy on the other side of the world. In colonial days it

took weeks before the country knew who had been elected president. Now we know before the election is over. Bad news travels just as fast. We gather more bad news in a day than the pioneers knew from the outside world in a year. A human spirit can take only so much news about murders, hijackings, floods, and terrorism without being distressed by the enormity of it all. How many people can we see dumped on the tarmac or sucked from a hole in the side of an airplane before—well, you see the kinds of assaults our minds must absorb if we allow all of this information to come in. All of this bad news is further frustrating because we are powerless to do anything about it.

In the place of bad news, read uplifting books. In the morning when I get up I have about a half hour alone when I can read something that fortifies me for the day. In the Bible Paul gives some instructions that have special benefit in our modern stressful world.

Finally brethren, whatever things are true, whatever things are noble, whatever things are just, whatever things are pure, whatever things are lovely, whatever things are of good report, if there is any virtue and if there is anything praiseworthy—meditate on these things (Philippians 4:8 NKJV).

4. **Avoid conflicts.** We can't always avoid conflicts, but some people are careless about getting into them. They seem unable to understand how they constantly bring conflicts into their own lives. Some conflicts, of course, can be avoided only by removing ourselves entirely from the person or situation involved.

If the conflict causes you to become upset or excited, the adrenal glands and several others begin to work overtime preparing the body for fight or flight. Since it is unlikely that you will either get in a fight or run away, your body will simply be revved up and stressed out for nothing.

Indecision is another form of conflict. Messies have a lot of that. Since we are perfectionists and always want to make the right decision, we spend a lot of time and energy wrestling with each choice. Wrestling is exhausting. And we do it over every little thing. When I first began to get rid of excess possessions I could only do it for an hour or so a day because the decision-making wore me out. I wanted to keep the things, but I knew I could not live the way I wanted to with so much stuff in my house. I was under a lot of pressure and my body felt it.

In her book *Women and Fatigue* Holly Atkinson says, "Conflicts ... are a major source of fatigue in women. Such conscious or unconscious struggles between two opposing desires or courses of action keep the brain working overtime, which uses more energy."

5. **Take control of your time and your house.** There are two major ways to do this. First, take the role of an authoritative person. If your attitude is passive and pliable, others will control your life and you will be frustrated, stressed, and tired. But if you have confidence that your thoughts, desires, and plans are worthwhile and productive, it will show in the way you stand, speak, and conduct yourself. People will respect you and your plans. You will not always be right, but you will be in control. This will relieve the stress of helplessness.

As you change from being non-assertive to assertive, those around you will go through four stages of adjustment. Our country went through these stages when faced with the civil rights movement and the Vietnam protests. They were also the stages the church went through in the first century. So don't take it personally when you see it happening to you.

First, they will ignore you. They hope this is just a phase that will go away if they pretend it is unimportant.

Second, they will misinterpret it. They will say, "Mother is just not herself lately. Perhaps it is that time of month," or, "She's on another one of her improvement kicks again." They will say anything except, "Mother wants things to be different and she is certainly right."

Third, when they see that you won't back down, they will resist your desires with a certain sense of urgency. They will attack you for not letting things rock along as they have been. You may hear such statements as, "You are making a nuisance of yourself." "I will pick those things up in a little while." "Don't be such a grouch." "I wish you were the way you used to be." When this happens, just say to yourself, "Stage three."

Fourth, when they see that all of these approaches do not deter you, they will begin the final stage, cooperation. And you and they will be the better for it.

The second way of gaining control is to become proficient in what you do. If it is housekeeping, you know what to do and how to do it. Your house is under control because you are more powerful than it is. Your house, which up to this time has frustrated and humiliated you, is no longer a source of stress because you have found a stronger force—the power of ability. Just knowing you can control it helps relieve tension. The real tension will be relieved when the house is beautiful and orderly. Then the stress of an ugly house, so powerful because it is so close to the source of womanhood, will be alleviated.

We do not want to lead stress-free lives. Nothing is as boring as a do-nothing life that is so stress free we become flaccid. We need to find some cause or goal that encourages us to strive for excellence in some area.

Stress that is out of control weakens our lives. We become angry. We can't function well. We need to be strong, capable women to fulfill the plan for which we were put into the world. It is within our control if we are willing to make the changes necessary.

Ten Suggestions for Beating Stress

(I would call them commandments but I am not God, and besides, commandments might add to your stress.)

1. Accept your own imperfections and go ahead in spite of them.
2. Avoid fighting for anything that is not really worth it.
3. Don't squander your energy on semi-important things.
4. Say no more often.
5. Get rid of a lot.
6. Don't gather much.
7. Don't keep much.
8. Value simplicity in your life-style.
9. Don't sweat the little things.
   (Everything is a little thing.)
10. Be grateful.

Assess the Mess

1. List your biggest sources of stress.

   a.

   b.

   c.

2. Which of the ten suggestions will you use to help you overcome this stress?

   a.

   b.

   c.

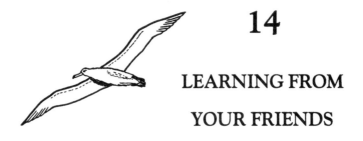

14

LEARNING FROM
YOUR FRIENDS

TIGGER, OUR CAT, had not been well so we took him to the vet. My husband wanted to carry Tigger in a cage but I assured him that I could handle the cat with no problem. Tigger rode quietly in my lap all the way to the vet's office, which is located on one of the busiest streets in Miami. Many cars that regularly drive on it wear bumper stickers with the slogan, "Pray for me. I drive on Bird Road." We knew we had to be careful getting the cat out of the car and into the vet's office. We parked as close to the door as possible. As soon as my husband opened the door on my side of the car and I stood up with the cat in my arms, our placid, cooperative animal became a maniac. Scratching my arms and grabbing with his back legs for my skirt to use as a push-off point, the cat flailed in all directions. My husband and I were flailing too, afraid to let go of the cat and afraid to hold him. Both of us tried to hold on to some part. Finally the cat was on the ground between two parked cars, and one of us, I don't remember which one, had hold of the frantic, fighting animal by only one foot. Our worst fears were about to come true.

In the midst of the melee, I sighted one more blur. A streak of white appeared, and the cat disappeared. When I gained my composure, I saw a young man in a long white lab coat standing on the sidewalk in front of the car holding an unhappy but very controlled cat in his arms. He was the vet's assistant.

I asked him later where he had come from. He had just stepped out of the office to help another owner carry his pet's cage to the car. He had seen our plight. The rest was obvious.

"All you have to do is hold him like this right on the back of his neck," he said, demonstrating. He was right. You just had to know how.

Like Tigger, our houses get totally out of control sometimes. We think we can handle it alone, but despite our confidence and best plans, we can't.

At these times we need to bring in professional help—either a book or a professional organizer who will come to our home, grab our whirlwind by the scruff of the neck, and say, "Here's how."

Sometimes we don't have to go far. We can learn from our friends and neighbors who have orderly homes but don't seem to work at it.

Every quantifiable aspect of life can be divided into three parts: height can be divided into short, average, and tall; weight into skinny, average, and fat; the way we eat into anorexic, normal, and overeater. In the same way, housekeeping skills can be divided into Messie, Average, and Cleanie. Like the anorexic and overeater who both have an eating problem, Cleanies and Messies both have a cleaning problem. Both have a compulsion to control things.

The Cleanie is visually sensitive. She wants to have visual things under her control. She cannot stand the sight of clutter or dirt. Everything has its place, usually out of sight, and she makes sure it stays there so she can find it when she wants it. Her area of responsibility is narrow and well-defined. She works hard and long. She keeps a tight rein on her household. This puts great stress on her family because living in such a house is never relaxing.

The Messie also wishes to be in control but she takes a different approach. She keeps everything in sight so she will have it when she needs it. She keeps a lot of things she is unlikely to need because, as she says, "You never know. Someone might need it someday." This great bulk of material, much of it sitting out so she can keep an eye on it, is a great distress to her family and to herself as well. The house is not pleasant to live in and it does not look good. Nobody can find things, the house is hard to clean, and the family is embarrassed to invite people over. The Messie feels as if she works hard all the time but accomplishes little.

You just have to know how to do it.

The average housekeeper does not have a housekeeping problem. She blithely goes along with a pleasant house. She takes pride and pleasure in her house, but she doesn't work at housekeeping very much. Those of us who are frazzled Messies wonder when she does it. She seems to spend her hours doing pleasant things, such as having coffee with friends or going out. The pleasant house is important to her. The housekeeping is not. She knows she is not perfect and she is comfortable with that fact. She is average but she is successful.

That is what we are going to aim for—to be a successful average housekeeper. We do not want to trade being a Messie for being a Cleanie any more than an overweight person wants to trade overeating for anorexia.

MESSIE	AVERAGE	CLEANIE
1	5	10

Put an arrow at the point where you are now. Then draw a stick figure where you wish to be. Put a smiley face on the figure while you are doing it. Think of how nice it will be to live that kind of life.

To find out how successful average housekeepers keep their houses nice without much effort, I interviewed some women I had known for several years. To determine if they were successful average housekeepers, I used two criteria: (1) Over a period of years were their houses consistently in good order when I visited, with or without prior notice? (2) Did they show a marked disinterest in housekeeping?

When I interviewed Cleanies for a previous book, *The Messies Manual*, I thought Cleanies seemed rather detached about housekeeping. But once I got them going, they began to tell me their schedules, attitudes, tricks, techniques, etc., which were legion.

In contrast, the successful average housekeepers I interviewed never really warmed up to the subject. They downgraded the importance of the whole thing. Housekeeping was not their number-one priority. They were consistent in saying they liked to have a nice house, but they were also consistently casual about how they accomplished it. When pushed they said they cleaned routinely. "I just do it to get it done," said one. "It's just a routine, you know," said another. One said that she enjoyed cleaning. Another said that she liked her house and she enjoyed taking care of it. They did not spend much time doing housework. Perhaps five hours a week to clean and organize closets, cupboards, etc. I told one woman that I had heard of someone who could clean her house in two hours a week. Apparently unimpressed and distracted by the party she was hosting at the time, she mumbled, "Forty-five minutes would be more like it."

I interviewed women from many circumstances, from a retiree who lived alone in a three-bedroom, one-bath house to a woman who worked part-time and lived with five people, three generations, in the same size house as the single retiree. These women all lived in South Florida, where the houses are small and the yards large because people spend more of their time outside. But their attitudes apply universally.

1. **Successful housekeepers want their houses to look nice.** They do not keep a nice house so it will work well, so they can find

things, or so they can store things. Repeatedly they say they want the house to look good.

Messies usually want the house to work well. At one seminar I asked the participants why they wanted to get their houses in order. All who answered gave practical reasons: "So I can find things," "So I won't be embarrassed," "So I can get my kids off to school without so much hassle," and, "So I won't have to work so hard." One woman timidly raised her hand, "Would it be all right to say I want my house to look like *Better Homes and Gardens?*"

Her answer hit the heart of the reason successful average housekeepers keep the house nice. People who want their houses to look nice end up having houses that work well and people who want their houses to work well end up with houses that don't work *or* look nice. The reason for this is that beauty is more powerful than practicality. A captivating vision of a lovely home will pull a reforming Messie much further along than the urge to have a working home will push her.

Like the anorexic and overeater who both have
an eating problem, Cleanies and Messies
both have a cleaning problem.

---

2. Successful housekeepers are nice to themselves. They believe they deserve a nice house and that it is okay for them to have what they need and want. They do not deny themselves as Messies do. They may go without something because they do not have the money to get it, but they do not do it out of principle.

3. Successful housekeepers trust their feelings. They have good instincts about what to keep and what to get rid of. They are a great deal more casual than Messies when it comes to things in the house. They do not LOVE things the way Messies do. They do not FEAR making a mistake, not having an important item, or giving away something they will want later.

What really amazed me when I was talking to them were their relationships to their collections. One had a collection of clown figurines and pictures. As I looked around her house I saw that the shelf of clown figurines seemed to be full. "What will you do with other figurines you may get?" I asked. "I've stopped collecting them," she replied. I was amazed. I didn't know you could stop a collection when you ran out of space. I thought a collection was like a friendship. You kept it up even if it became inconvenient.

Another woman who had a collection of blue glass said the same thing. She was about to stop collecting it because her window ledge was filling up.

They also have casual feelings about books and magazines. Those who love and receive magazines regularly enjoy reading them and sharing them with friends. They keep them as long as they wish and then throw them away or take them to the Laundromat, beauty parlor, or a neighbor.

When I asked these successful average housekeepers if they kept the bottom portion of bills after paying them (the part that says "Keep this portion for your own records") some did but most did not. They said the canceled check was enough. This was amazing to me since the stub says very clearly what to do with it. I have always been happy to keep the stubs and probably would have kept them even if I'd never been instructed to do so. These are cavalier people who live dangerously. I'll bet they even remove the tag from pillows that says "Do not remove under penalty of law."

On the other hand, they keep whatever they want and buy whatever they need, within the limits of their finances of course. This freedom spares them from the sense of impending deprivation that makes Messies want to keep everything.

The Book of Proverbs has an interesting comment on this phenomenon, "It is possible to give away and become richer! It is also possible to hold on too tightly and lose everything. Yes, the liberal man shall be rich! By watering others, he waters himself" (11:24–25 TLB).

Is this not true of the situation we are describing? Those who willingly give things away gain a beautiful, orderly house. Those who hold on to everything lose what they are hoarding, the peace and comfort of ownership.

The point I am making is that successful average housekeepers are not driven by their emotions in such a way that love or fear binds them to keep something. They are emotionally detached, whether keeping or buying. This detachment gives them the freedom to decide wisely.

Two successful average housekeepers I interviewed stressed the importance of moderation. One said, "I do things in moderation. I don't want to be a fanatic. It makes a person too tense." The other said, "Moderation is the key word with everything."

4. Successful housekeepers are alert to the house. They know when it is cluttered, full, empty, pretty, etc. Unlike the Messie, the successful housekeeper has a feeling for the condition of the house. It is similar to hunger and fullness. People who overeat are often unaware of when they are hungry or full, so they eat inappropriately. A normal person eats when hungry and stops when full. The overweight person eats out of habit, without thought of hunger, without tasting her food. The normal person is aware of the taste and amount of food she takes in.

In a similar way, Messies function as machines when it comes to the house. They do many destructive things without realizing the negative impact they will have. The mail is a good example. Messies frequently put it in a pile on a table with little thought or care. They keep it, junk and all, as a matter of course. They also keep receipts and coupons mindlessly.

Here are some techniques to help you decide what to keep until you break the "keep everything" habit.

a. **Be aware of the things happening in the house.** When you want to buy something, especially something big, do not do so until you know where to put it. For a day or two before you buy it, visualize where it will go and how it will fit in.

b. **Rate the things you're not sure whether or not you should keep.** Pick a closet or a drawer and sort everything in it into three piles. If you really want or need something put it in pile 1 and put it neatly where it belongs when you finish this exercise. If you are ambivalent about something, put it in pile 2, store it in an ambivalence box, and put today's date on it. Whatever you don't use in the next month, get rid of. Put the things you don't need into pile 3 and give them to a good cause or throw them away.

When saving becomes a conscious decision rather than an automatic reflex your house will have a lot less clutter. If while cleaning the closet you find a piece of clothing you don't like at all, put it in pile 3 and get rid of it. If you're going through your mail drawer and find an advertisement about rifles and you've never hunted in your life, put it in pile 3. If you're saving it for a friend who hunts, address an envelope to him and put it in the mail. Do not set it down again.

The condition of your house depends on your ability to make decisions about your clutter. A decision delayed is a decision unmade, and a decision unmade lets clutter invade.

In the past you kept things because you had a vague feeling they might be good for something someday. You were an automatic saving machine. Now the automatic part has been turned off and you have taken control of what you keep and what you get rid of.

"It is possible to give away and become richer!
It is also possible to hold on too tightly
and lose everything."

---

5. **Successful housekeepers live in the present.** This characteristic has broad implications. Because they do not live in, think about, or worry much about the past, they do not keep much memorabilia, including receipts, stubs, or old trophies. Not one person I interviewed had a file cabinet, not even a one-drawer cabinet or file box. All of them had a small drawer for their papers. One kept insisting that she did have a file. It was a little accordion style divider folder about the size of a business envelope. In it she kept all of her important papers and her records about bills. She could hold it in her hand and she kept it in a drawer. One woman had a box at a bank where she kept such things as birth certificates and mortgages.

The reason Messies are more likely to have big file cabinets may be symbolic. File cabinets symbolize order, and Messies, recognizing their need for this illusive quality, probably figure "the bigger the better." So they buy a big file cabinet and wait for it to organize their lives. Instead it becomes another place of disorder. It may be a slight improvement. Now the papers are all in one place. But even that advantage is debatable because sometimes it's easier to find papers among books, magazines, and newspapers than it is to find a particular paper among an array of similar-looking papers.

Another advantage of living in the present is not always having to plan for the future. I was amazed at how these women did projects without long-range planning. One had just redone her bathroom. It was absolutely breathtaking with black tub, toilet, and sink, light gray tile, and lots of mirrors. I asked her how they had planned it. Had they looked at a lot of magazines on bathrooms? Had they shopped a lot for the best prices? Had they received professional advice?

No, they had gone to a showroom, gotten their brochure, and called to ask the prices of the items they selected. They had them installed by a carpenter who had no opinions and offered no advice but loved the bathroom when it was finished. They did not have a file full of ideas before they began. They did not plan long ahead.

This lack of long-range planning—for hobbies, travel, decorating, or whatever—was consistent among successful average housekeepers. When they wanted to do something they knew where to find the necessary information. A number of them had just remodeled their homes. They all did it the same way—by going to a few stores until they saw what they liked. They all seemed happy with their choices.

Messies, on the other hand, frequently have many big projects on the burner for some time in the undetermined future. They hoard brochures and magazines, fearing that when the time comes to do the project they will not know what they want or where to get it. I believe some Messies over-plan because they don't think they will ever accomplish their plans. Collecting things is a sub-conscious wish to participate in what they do not really expect will happen. In the end, the Messies who plan so diligently are frequently less successful than those who do not plan much at all.

Successful average housekeepers are not particularly fearful. They do not worry that some forgetfulness from the past will come back to haunt them. They are confident of their own tastes. They don't have a lot of partially finished projects lying around, so they don't fear starting new ones. They do not fear the future, so they don't keep things they may need someday.

The successful average housekeeper mentality.

It is not enough for us to see what successful average housekeepers do; we must catch the feeling of how they think. They are optimistic and fearless when it comes to housekeeping. They are confident of their own tastes and power over the house. They live in the present and do not hang on to the past. Their lives are so fulfilling that they are not afraid of being shortchanged.

In *Diets Don't Work* author Bob Schwartz suggests that his readers approach food the way a thin person does. We can take a clue from this exercise and learn to approach our belongings the way a successful average housekeeper does, using that same op-timism, detachment, resolve, and desire.

Changing is like being a trapeze artist. She swings into mid-air holding a bar. Back and forth she swings, higher and higher. As soon as she gets high enough she lets go of the bar and catches one coming from the opposite direction. To get to the other bar she must let go of the first. This is the way it is when you let go of the old way of thinking. Making the change is scary, but if you want to get to the new bar, you have to let go of the old one.

Assess the Mess

1. These are my worst fears about what would happen if I detached myself from the things in my house.

    a.

    b.

    c.

    d.

2. These are the activities I would like to change in my life (e.g., I would stop keeping magazines that are years old).

    I would stop ...

    I would start ...

3. Some of the things that detract from the beauty of my home are:

    a.

    b.

    c.

    d.

4. The thinking patterns I need to let go of are:

    a.

    b.

    c.

    d.

5. The thinking patterns I need to take hold of are:

   a.

   b.

   c.

   d.

   Perhaps you think you could profit from some outside professional help to zero in on how you can improve the organization of your home. Before I give the address of the National Association of Professional Organizers, I want to remind you that the problem is not your house; it's your mindset. Until that is changed there will be no permanent change in your house no matter how many professionals you hire. If professional organizers get your house in perfect order before you change your mindset, the house will slip back into its former condition. For a list of professional organizers write:

   National Association of Professional Organizers
   5350 Wilshire Boulevard
   P.O. Box 36E02
   Los Angeles, CA 90036

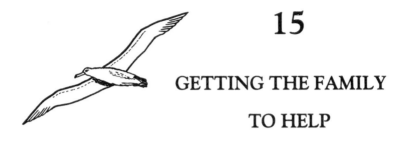

15

GETTING THE FAMILY

TO HELP

MESSIES HAVE VARYING home backgrounds as far as housekeeping is concerned. Some had meticulous mothers. They kept the house in order at all times. Housekeeping was their hobby and career combined. The little Messie child came into this orderly world and neither Mom nor Messie could figure out what was happening. The child and the Mom were in repeated conflict. Mom won most of the time. Sometimes the child grew up hating the thing that caused so much of her childhood trouble, that superorderly house.

Some had moms who were Messies, too. Messie Mom and Messie child had a tough time fighting the house together, and sometimes each blamed the other for being the source of the trouble. In desperation Mom would look to the child to help more than any child, especially a Messie child, could. This Messie child also grew up hating the house, the source of conflict and, in relation to her friends, embarrassment.

Most Messies were probably brought up in an average household where the mom was confident of her own ability to keep things under control and didn't make a big thing of it. She was flexible, but only to a point. The little Messie grew up with her mess controlled but without being unduly pressured about the house.

She may not have realized the extent of her messy problem. This is the child who is surprised that housekeeping is hard for her. Mom never made a big deal of it and everything was fine. But when she doesn't make a big deal over keeping house, the whole thing goes to pot.

Your Family Now

A recovering Messie needs the help of the family to solve the problem of an out-of-control house. You need them to support you in the change you are making in yourself. You also need them to cooperate with you in your plans. The first is negotiable; the second, within limits, is not.

Support

You may have a number of personal relationships to consider when you think about your family and the house. Whatever their opinions about the change in your life, you need to talk clearly to them about the support you want from them. They may or may not be sympathetic. If they are, that is a help for you. If they are not, you will continue with your change and perhaps later they will understand and offer their support.

There are four reasons why the family of the Messie may resist the change.

First, some spouses subconsciously resist because they are used to being the superior person in regard to the house. They have gotten into the habit of fussing at the Messie and of telling her what to do around the house. When the Messie begins to take control, that area of dominance begins to disappear and the husband may resent it.

Second, some spouses feel as if they have lost a trump card in the relationship. If the husband used the messiness of the house as an excuse for requiring other things from his wife to compensate, he will no longer be able to demand these "extras."

Third, the husband himself may have been using the condition of the house as an excuse for not doing certain things, such as entertaining.

You're not searching for perfection.
You do not want to turn into a shrew
who makes coming home miserable.

Fourth, the husband may have been blaming his wife for the total problem of messiness. If she changes, it will become obvious that he and other members of the family are not innocent victims of Mom's problem.

Keep in mind these reasons for resistance when you explain to your family your need for their support. Frequently they are not aware of their own resistance. Ask clearly for their support and together work through the problems that arise.

Cooperation

The area of cooperation is not negotiable. Your family will have to do their part in the house. Care must be taken here. You are not searching for perfection. You do not want to turn into a shrew who makes coming home miserable. When you make changes in what you expect from them they will have some long-established habits to break.

You may also have a dyed-in-the-wool Messie child who is afraid to change, afraid to get rid of his or her personal clutter. When you are working against this compulsive fear, you need to be understanding—but firm.

Successful average housekeepers expect their families to cooperate and, in most cases, people do what is expected of them. One of the successful average housekeepers I spoke to had three rules for her family:

1. Remove your dirty dishes from the table, rinse them, and put them in the dishwasher.

2. Put your dirty clothes and towels in the hamper.

3. Wipe the shower wall after a shower (a must).

From time to time she asks them to do a few other jobs, like folding clothes from the dryer or unloading the dishwasher. Her opinion is that if they know they are going to be part of cleaning up, they will be more careful about messing up and they will share more fully in the pride of having a lovely home.

Assess the Mess

1. Who will you need to talk to about supporting your change?

  a.

  b.

  c.

  d.

  e.

2. When will you talk to each of them?

3. What strategy will you use to convince them of the importance of their cooperation?

4. List the names of people whose cooperation you need for success. Beside their names, write the tasks you want them to do.

Names   **Tasks You Want Them to Do**

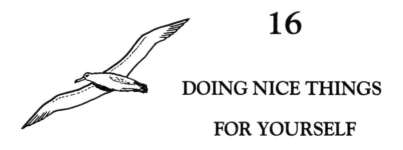

16

DOING NICE THINGS

FOR YOURSELF

FORMER PRESIDENT REAGAN'S daughter Maureen and I agreed in a telephone interview that we did not make any improvements in the house if it required more than five minutes and more than a hammer to do. I mention this conversation because I like to drop famous names wherever possible, as you may know if you read my third book, *The Messies SuperGuide*, in which I was even able to work in the name of the Queen of England in relation to Messies Anonymous.

I also mention it to introduce the kind of helpful hints you will find in my books. Most of them are simple to do. It is not that I disapprove of the others; I just don't do them. At the end of this chapter I will mention books with suggestions that require more extensive use of time and tools. I am not very handy with tools, but I am better than my husband. When work needs to be done around the house I hire a local husband who wants to make a little extra money by doing a few odd jobs. My husband doesn't mind if someone else does it as long as he's not in town. I found this out when he got back after the first time I nervously did it.

Most of the suggestions I make here are easy and quick to do.

The Telephone Area

Did you ever hear a frustrated voice at the other end of the telephone line saying, "Just a minute. This pen doesn't work. The pen at my phone never works. Phil, will you hand me that pen! Just a minute. *Phil*, my pen doesn't work! Hand me a pen or a pencil! O.K. O.K. Now I'm ready. Go ahead."

Perhaps you were the frustrated voice at the end of the line. And once you found a pen, where did you write the message? And where did you put the message after writing it? The telephone message center is often one of the most confused areas in the disorganized household, and it is one of the easiest to get organized. Do yourself a favor and organize your phone center. You need only a few basic items.

The first is the aforementioned pen. Buy one that sticks to the side of the phone with a coiled wire or chain. That way no one can pick it up and take it away "for just a minute" and fail to return it. Frequently you can find a pen to coordinate with the phone color. Look in a variety store, an office supply store, or a drugstore.

The second piece of equipment you need is a spiral-bound notebook designed to take phone messages and record them in duplicate. The one I have will hold four hundred messages. The top copy tears out and the duplicate stays in the book. If someone calls and leaves a phone number for your husband, you write it in the book, tear out the top paper, and give it to him. If he loses it, you still have a record of it. You will be surprised at how often you refer to your permanent record. Keep this record book near the phone.

The third piece of equipment to buy is an address file. The Rolodex-type system I have comes in two sizes. I use the larger size, 3 x 5, because I put more than just telephone numbers and addresses on it. The one I use has no cover because taking it off is just one more hindrance to using the system easily. Mine sits right on top of the phone table.

The fourth piece of equipment you'll need is a telephone table to put the phone on or to put under the wall phone. Don't try to "make-do" without adequate storage space at the phone. This is

---

*The more junk we keep
the less effective our nurturing will be.
It gives the illusion of nurturing but little of the reality.*

---

particularly important for people who live in cities where there is more than one large phone book to contend with. Look for a phone table at odd places. Furniture stores may have them. I ordered mine from a mail-order catalog. The phone books and spiral-bound message book go in it.

Finally you need to buy two things for the phone—a long cord and a phone shoulder cradle. I have a twenty-five-foot long cord made by AT&T that I bought at an office supply discount store for about five dollars. It is easy to plug in on both ends. The phone cradle I'm talking about is not the foam type. It is made of hard plastic and has a longer attachment that lifts the phone to your ear. They can be found at Radio Shack and other places. These two things free you to do other things while you talk on the phone. One of the successful average housekeepers I talked to always picks up a damp cloth when she is on the phone and begins to wipe her kitchen. On long conversations, she polishes her brass things. Be nice to yourself. Make the phone center more convenient for you and your family.

The Kitchen Area

The main thing to be done to the kitchen is to unclutter it. By looking at things piece by piece we will be able to get the kitchen under control and in easy working order.

First of all, let's face it. The real problem in the kitchen is way, way, way too much junk. Some of it was given to us by older women at showers who should have known we'd never use it. Some we bought ourselves when we were young and foolish and thought we would need it. Some we bought when we were old and foolish. Women are suckers for anything that promises to make us better nurturers. That's why it is so hard to get rid of kitchen things. But the more junk we keep, the less effective our nurturing will be. It gives an illusion of nurturing but little of the reality.

Pack in boxes things you have not used for a while. On the boxes write a date about two months from when you pack it. You can retrieve things from the boxes until that date. Whatever you haven't retrieved by then, give to some charity.

Countertops

The top of the counter sets the stage for the atmosphere of the kitchen. If they are neat, the whole kitchen looks neat. To clear the countertop, look for ways to get as much off it as possible.

Under-the-cabinet appliances—such as coffee makers, can openers, toasters, broiler ovens, radios and televisions, microwave ovens, hand mixers, and blenders—are a great help in recovering lost counter space. Almost all small appliances can now be removed from valuable countertops. You must, however, make careful decisions as to what appliances to purchase for that purpose. After all, under-the-counter space is not limitless either.

Canisters, which are commonly kept on the counter, I keep inside the cabinets. Even though they are a set, I make no effort to keep them together. I put them in a cabinet nearest the place I usually use them. Don't stick your cooking spoons, spatulas, forks, etc., into a holder on the counter where they stick out like a metallic bouquet. Hang them from a specially designed hanger or keep them in a drawer. I hang my knives from a metallic bar mounted on the side of the cabinet.

If you are short on drawer space try the instant drawers made by Rubbermaid, available in hardware stores and other places. They fit under the cabinet as well. One of the things I have enjoyed most is the pull-down spice caddy, which also mounts (as if you could not have guessed it) under the cabinet. Finally, don't overlook shelf units that you install inside cabinet doors to hold kitchen stuff.

If you have run out of cabinet space, you can have a long, narrow shelf built between the countertop and the upper cabinet to hold many of the things previously on the counter. If your microwave oven takes up valuable counter space, look for a microwave oven cart that will fit the decor of your kitchen. These carts have the additional advantage of having more cabinet space below and frequently more shelf space above where you can store cookbooks or small appliances. If the microwave cord does not reach the proper outlet, buy a cart that rolls or use an air-conditioning extension cord.

On the countertop you may wish to put one flower pot with flowers. That's enough. This clear counter space, so easy for you to use and enjoy looking at, will inspire you to do more in the area of kitchen organization.

I could tell you to poke a hole in the center of a shower cap, stick your beaters through it, and use it to cover your mixing bowl when you use it. This eliminates splatters, but you're left with one really messy shower cap to clean. And where would you store such a thing? It is easier to be careful and to wipe up where you splatter.

I could also tell you to put your meat and candy thermometers into plastic eyeglass holders to keep them safe. Or to use plastic coffee lids between hamburger patties when you freeze them so you can pop them apart easily later. I could recommend that you cut small circles out of plastic lids and then cut an X in the center and use them as plastic bag closures. But if you did all these things you would be back in the saving-and-keeping syndrome, spending your time ruining scissors and your schedule by cutting out little circles. And where would you store the things? In another empty eyeglass holder? Eventually you would need a rack to hold all of the eyeglass holders.

The point I am making is that you should avoid the craziness of doing all of this extra stuff. A lot of these types of suggestions are very useful in making the kitchen easier to live in, but a recovering Messie can start getting so overorganized that she makes another mess. Get things set up in a reasonable way and don't go overboard. Often, especially in the kitchen, less is more.

The Refrigerator

There is probably no area in the house where being a Messie shows up as much as in the refrigerator. The Messie's refrigerator is ordinarily full of a variety of things in various kinds of containers and in various states of decomposition. Messies save scraps others

---

A recovering Messie can start getting so overorganized that she makes another mess. Get things set up in a reasonable way and don't go overboard.

---

throw away. Perhaps a kitten will wander up to the door and you will need something to feed him. So you save it "just in case." The refrigerator is also full because the Messie forgets what she puts in there. No one could remember all those odds and ends.

The successful housekeeper throws away more to begin with than the Messie. If you are a Messie who tends to have a messy refrigerator, try to put less in than you do. To keep track of leftovers purchase a small magnetic bulletin board with a wipe-off pen attached and write on it the name of the leftover and the date you put it in the refrigerator.

I suppose I should tell you to decide which shelves will hold which items (e.g., dairy products on the top shelf, leftovers and cold cuts on the second, etc.). This is a good idea but I have never been able to make it work. I keep forgetting which shelf is for what. In addition, sometimes the containers don't fit where they belong and I have to put them on an improper shelf. This drives a perfectionistic Messie to distraction.

Using small uncovered square basket containers is very helpful for grouping things. Condiments do much better in those little baskets. Without them the little jars get pushed to the back and are never seen again. When you finally get around to cleaning the refrigerator you'll find eight jars of pickle relish lined up against the back of the refrigerator interspersed with several half-used jars of mustard. Round those little rascals up in a basket and they'll stay put so you can find them.

I should also tell you to use square refrigerator containers for storage because they fit together better and waste less space. However, I don't want you to go out and buy loads of square containers so you can get more in the refrigerator. Messies already get too much in there. The answer is to find a balance. Keep as little as possible, but keep it efficiently.

Other areas you will need to consider when getting your house in order are the kid's rooms, bathrooms, and closets. I have already written about some of these in other books, and many others have written helpful books about these and other practical areas of housekeeping.

Books

General

Totally Organized the Bonnie McCullough Way, Bonnie Mc-
Cullough, 1986, St. Martin's Press. This is one of my favorite books.
It covers many topics in a practical way and includes a section on
organizing and working with children, which is very helpful.

It's Here ... Somewhere, Alice Fulton and Pauline Hatch, 1985,
Writer's Digest Books. This is a nicely presented book that includes
room-by-room decorating tips, including the garage and porch.

How to Get Organized When You Don't Have the Time, Stephanie
Culp, 1986, Writer's Digest Books. This book deals in a balanced
way with two areas of organization: time and space. It has a unique
section on organizing the car and one on helping other people get
organized. She tells a scary story about how bad disorganization can
be. It might make some Messies nervous.

Confessions of an Organized Housewife and *Escape from the
Kitchen*, Deniece Schofield, 1982 and 1986, Writer's Digest Books.
These books are both a little stiff for fun-loving Messies, but if you
read them for the information and don't let the seriousness get to
you they will be helpful. They are particularly good on storage
ideas. The first one has a chapter on storing toys and one on arts
and crafts storage.

The Messies Manual (the basis of the Messies Anonymous approach), *Messies 2* (how to get yourself under control), and *The
Messies Superguide* (which deals further with the Messie problem
and has a special section written by an interior decorator who is a
Messie), Sandra Felton, Fleming H. Revell. Each has a special
emphasis on some aspect of the Messie mentality.

Special Topics

Taming the Paper Tiger: Organizing the Paper in Your Life, Barbara
Hamphill, 1988, Dodd, Mead and Company, Inc. This is an excellent book on problems with papers in the home. Like all good books
it offers not only "hows" but "whys." Of course, the best idea is not
to have so many papers. But she will help you with that, too.

The Compleat Garage Sale Book, Jeff Groberman and Colin Yardley, 1987, Prima Publishing and Communications. This book tells you everything you could ever want to know about garage sales. Get your overflow moving profitably out of your house and into someone else's.

76 Ways to Get Organized for Christmas, Bonnie McCullough and Bev Cooper, 1982, St. Martin's Press. Christmas requires so much organization and is so stressful for disorganized people that this book, by the same Bonnie who wrote *Totally Organized,* has got to be of some help.

How to Organize Your Kid's Room, Susan Isaacs, 1985, Ballantine Books. This is a super-good book on the subject. It was refreshing and enlightening to me. I think it would be good for any of you who have kids and want help for helping them in their rooms.

You can read these books for free by checking them out of your public library or by finding a quiet corner in your local bookstore. I like to read at least one of them a year. By the way, the books I have written are sometimes found in the religious section of the bookstore because my publisher publishes religious books as well as some on more general topics. Sometimes my books are found in the humor section.

In addition to books, many women's magazines are excellent sources for information on the kitchen and the three areas I mentioned. They often have better visual presentations than books because they use large colored pictures along with their written material.

By the time you read this book there will be several other excellent ones you will want to get. You can also order many of the latest books from Messies Anonymous. We try to keep up with books that meet the Messie's needs and to make them available through our catalog. Our address is:

Messies Anonymous
Department M
5025 S.W. 114th Avenue
Miami, FL 33165

17

ORGANIZING

YOUR TIME

THERE IS NO SENSE beating around the bush when talking about time management. There are three basic things you need to manage your time well.

A Goal

One of the basic tenets of this book is that Messies frequently are foggy about what they really want to do. They are pushed by external forces without zeroing in on what they themselves want to do. This confusion, I believe, accounts for the fragmentation in the way Messies use their time. Unable to decide what kind of life they want to lead, they cannot take control of their time to create that kind of life.

> "Would you tell me, please, which way I ought to go from here?" asked Alice.
> "That depends a good deal on where you want to go," said the Cat.
> "I don't much care where," said Alice.
> "Then it doesn't matter which way you go," said the Cat.

We are somewhat like Alice in her conversation with the Cheshire Cat in Lewis Carroll's *Alice in Wonderland.* We have not decided where we want to go.

Now is a good time to make that decision. Decide which way you want to go in the following areas. Put your goals in usable form. After you write them, you will know better how to organize your time to get there.

1. Personal Development
2. Husband
3. Children
4. Education
5. Social Life
6. Career
7. Spiritual
8. House
9. Other

Take a moment to go over the list. Put a 1 by those that are most important to you and a 3 by the ones that are least important. All the rest are 2 and are of medium importance.

A Plan

Second, you need a plan to help you achieve your goals. If one of your goals is to write a book, part of your plan might be to get up an hour earlier every morning and write while the house is still quiet.

Your plan should include everything you need to do to remove obstacles from your path. If your social goal is to invite a different couple from church to your home every month, your plan should include who is responsible for cleaning which parts of the house, when it will be done, what you will serve, and when you will shop for groceries.

A Record

To record all this information, buy yourself a notebook that includes a place for your goals, plans, to-do and to-buy lists, appointments, and addresses. It should be small enough to fit into your purse so you don't have to carry something extra. It may be self-made from a small notebook bought at the drugstore or it may be a specially made leather notebook available in office supply stores.

If regularly used, this book will keep you going in the right direction. The fact that it puts information in writing gives it more significance. Poor planning and distractibility are held in check when we see our plans in black and white.

The Messie needs to realize that she may have a fluctuating relationship with her organizational book. The book tends to require linear, step-by-step thinking. Messies don't naturally think that way. They tend to think in ways built on stops, starts, circles, and unpredictable insights. The "to-do" list helps balance that kind of thinking, but it also causes some tension in the Messie's relationship with the book. The Messie may find that the "to-do" list floats in and out of importance. When a Messie is doing a creative mental task that does not require step-by-step functioning, the list may take a minor place. When she is doing some kind of mechanical task that requires monitoring and scheduling, such as redecorating some part of the house, the book figures prominently.

Once you have several goals and plans recorded you can begin to take control of your time. Without goals and plans, time will control itself.

My uncle owned a plantation that used mules for power even though tractors were available. We think of mules as animals that stubbornly stand still when we want them to move. But that was not all they did. They also moved when they were supposed to stand still, and usually in the wrong direction. And woe to anyone who got in an open field with them when they were loose. I'm convinced that all their laziness was an act to put people off guard so they could trample them to death. I still carry in my mind the picture of rough men wrestling with unruly mules. After the men convinced the mules that the men were in control, the mules would settle down and do the work. But each day the men had to go through the same steps. The point is that the people who worked with those mules had to keep them under tight control or they would go their own way and not do any work.

That's the way time is. It has a mind of its own. If we don't control it, it will take off, dragging us behind it. And we'll be flailing our arms and screaming that we don't have enough time to do what needs to be done. Time takes on a life and will of its own if we do not harness it to our plans and get it to accomplish our goals.

To harness time to our plans we have to unharness it from our faulty ways of thinking. This means letting go of some things to take hold of what is best.

Letting Go of Impulsiveness

Messies don't like to plan ahead. They prefer spontaneity. They like to act on impulse. Some Messies plan meals the day they plan to eat them because they don't know ahead of time what they'll feel like eating.

As I mentioned earlier, Messies work more on the basis of emotion than do other people. They wait to get into the mood to do something. This kind of impulsiveness, though healthy in small doses, cuts the heart out of a time-saving plan. No one expects a Messie to give up all spontaneity, but it's the kind of thing that only has value when used in moderation.

Because Messies are spur-of-the-moment people, they're often thought to have poor memories. But it's not so much that they forget things, they just don't take the time to think of them. They often waste time making extra trips to the store because they forgot to buy something. What they really neglected to do was make a list before they went the first time. Learning to write things down will help solve this problem and save a bundle of time.

Letting Go of Helpfulness

Being very altruistic, Messies let time get out of control when they help other people. Frequently these other people are their own families. After two days off work, your son John has to be back on the job at a local fast-food restaurant by four o'clock. At two he tells you that his uniform needs to be washed, dried, and ironed. It is possible, by dropping everything else you had planned to do, to get it done, and that's what John expects you to do.

Mary has a school project due tomorrow. At seven o'clock in the evening she tells you she needs poster board and some Magic Markers. She says she forgot until just now. She expects you to get in the car and go fetch them.

Time has a mind of its own.
If we don't control it, it will take off,
dragging us behind it.

These children have learned from previous experience that their mother, in her kindness, will cooperate with this kind of thoughtless behavior. Don't forget the part the Messie herself plays in this kind of behavior. She may actually get satisfaction from rescuing people. It makes her feel needed.

Messies who have gotten themselves into this trap should learn this motto:

> Lack of preparation on your part
> Does not necessarily constitute
> an emergency on my part.

This would make a nice sign for the family mentioned above. At least they would be forewarned. The soft-hearted Messie must learn to stand behind her resolve and not constantly bail the children out of situations they have created.

Solving the problem is more difficult when it's Dad doing the demanding. He has his wife running all kinds of last-minute errands that could have been done earlier if he had just thought ahead. As mentioned earlier, Messies do this kind of thing to themselves as well. It's called lack of preparation. They don't think about what they will need for a job until they start it. All of this errand running and preparing in spurts cuts into time severely. This confusion could be cut to almost nothing with forethought. But instead confused thinking leads to chaotic living and thoughtless, confused people. When we learn to refuse to help every desperate procrastinator, we'll be one step closer to curing our need to feel needed.

Letting Go of Perfectionism

Perfectionism is a big time waster. There is nothing wrong with doing things well, but the unrealistic demands Messies put on themselves make it impossible for them to get anything done. "Do it right or not at all" is their motto. But what the Messie means by "doing it right" is quite different from what an average person means. For an average person, cleaning the pantry might mean removing everything, wiping the shelves, throwing away what's old, and putting everything back in with like foods together. The Messie would do all of that and more. She would painstakingly wash every jar, can, and box; she would ponder over whether the Jell-O belonged on the dessert or salad shelf; and she would alphabetize all the fruits, vegetables, spices, and soups. This is not only time-consuming but complicated because the Messie also likes to keep cans of the same size and brand together, so sometimes her elaborate systems conflict with one another. Messies don't need higher standards for themselves; they need lower ones. Messies need to learn to say no and turn their heads when they see perfectionism winking at them from a messy cupboard.

In spite of the tendencies Messies have to lose control of their time, many of us have learned that it's possible to get it under control and use it to accomplish our goals. In addition to the things we need to let go of there are several things we need to take hold of before we can harness time to accomplish our goals.

Taking Hold of Mood Swings

Mood swings affect productivity. For weeks or months a Messie may rely heavily on her "to-do" list. But one day its usefulness wanes inexplicably, and the Messie drifts into a slower, less-organized, pattern of life. Good and useful habits go on vacation. Old disorganized ways return. At this time it is important for the Messie to remember several things.

1. **Don't make long-term commitments.** Since I know these swings come, I try not to make long-term commitments that require more constancy than I have. At the moment I am very interested in physical fitness. I enjoy exercising at a fitness center in our area. I realize, however, that I am changeable. No matter how committed I am now, that commitment may change whether I want it to or not. When the time came to sign up for one year or two, I signed up for one because I know that after a year I may feel differently. If I am still interested, I will sign up for another year. If not, I'll wait for my interest to return and then sign up again. When we know and accept ourselves, we can make more workable decisions.

I admire people who have more control than I do over their interests. I wish I were more that way. But there is nothing wrong with fluctuating personal interests. We are free to change them without worry. Long-range responsibilities are another matter, of course, and we stick with them through thick and thin.

2. **Accept the swings.** They are part of a natural pattern, and they have a purpose. Sometimes they signal the beginning of a creative period. Sometimes they are just a rest period so that the Messie can return refreshed to the more organized way of life. Don't be discouraged or feel as though you are failing. The organized pattern will return soon enough, stimulating you to a more productive orderliness.

3. **Control the swing.** Let some things go if you must but try to hold on to the basic habits and commitments. The longer a Messie lives in an orderly way, the less these swings to casual living will affect the order and beauty of her life.

Taking Hold of Dignity

Life is changeable in many ways but one constant must remain. Messies, like others, are people of dignity and worth. Just because we take a different approach to organization does not change that. Do not get down on yourself because you are not as consistent as you would like to be.

In addition to mood swings, there are other cyclical ebbs and flows that we must respect to fulfill our goals. There is the cycle of family life. There are times when women have tremendous stress put on them. I am convinced that men on the whole never have to deal with the amount or intensity of stress that women deal with, especially during the child-bearing years.

---

*Messies don't need
higher standards for themselves;
they need lower ones.*

The menstrual cycle, pregnancy, lactation, and menopause are physical stresses peculiar to women. The stress of caring for babies and young children, being the primary caregiver for school-age children, caring for a husband's needs, doing housework, and sometimes balancing a career are psychological and physical stresses that fall specifically on the woman's shoulders.

Hopefully, the husband will help with these tasks, but statistics show that seldom will he do even half of the work that relates to family life even during times of special stress in the woman's life. There is some indication that more husbands are sharing the work load today than previously. Those who do have husbands who understand and help should be especially grateful. In the years when the children are young, this help can make the difference between peace and chaos.

When a woman has young children, she needs to realize that this is a special cycle in her life. Her chief responsibility lies with them. But she has got to make room in her life for the house as well because she will be under even more stress if she allows the demands of her children to force her into keeping a messy house. There is only one thing harder than trying to keep a neat house in a family with young children: trying to live in a disorganized house with young children.

Having said this, however, it is important to realize that at this time of life we cannot expect to have as much control over our house or time as when our children are older or gone. A single mother who works has the greatest stress of all, except perhaps for the mother who works and has a husband who not only doesn't help but is twice as messy as the children. And you can't spank him!

If you find that your life is totally out of control and you suspect that it is your responsibility to your children that has thrown it out of whack, find some of your friends who have the same family situation as yours but who seem to be paddling smoothly down the stream you are drowning in. Discover some of their techniques and draw strength from the fact that it can be done.

Another cycle to be aware of is your own daily time clock. Some of us are morning people. Some are night people. Some are alert in the morning and evening but sluggish in the afternoon. We're all different. Try to use your peak time for hard jobs and decision making. Use your sluggish times to do things that do not require decisions or zip.

For a woman there is also the cycle of her periods. Be kind and demand less of yourself when your hormones are doing funny things to your moods and energy.

Try to find your natural rhythms and live in harmony with them. You may be concerned that you will neglect your responsibilities and blow your time schedule if you don't make yourself keep going in spite of whatever cycle you're in. Don't think this way. Treat yourself in a kind and understanding way and the well-being you feel will give you back more energy and enthusiasm than you would ever get by gritting your teeth and trudging doggedly forward.

In this same vein, respect your limitations and interests. You are unique. You have a special contribution to make. Let go of the optional responsibilities that are not in keeping with your interests and abilities. If you have to strain to do a certain job and if you don't like it very much you probably have no business doing it (if the choice is optional). You may wish to replace it with something more to your liking or you may wish to leave that time open to relieve strain from other activities.

Even though we can do much to right ourselves and avoid the fever of a confused life, in the end true order and beauty flow only from God, who made them both and said that they were good. James encourages us to ask God for wisdom and He will give it liberally. This does not apply to household hints, of course. God does not whisper to us that if we put our S.O.S. pads in a porous earthenware container they will not rust. He orders our steps by giving us the wisdom we need to balance our lives rightly.

There are many women who, because of their relationship with Him, have made their lives busier and have wearied themselves and their families with outside activity. I don't want to take away from the importance of working in God's vineyard, where there are not enough laborers. But before we do any kind of activity, organizing our houses, streamlining our use of time, doing important activities outside the home, engaging in important family activities, or working in that all-important vineyard, we need to pause and center ourselves. An uncentered wheel may go forward, but it is wobbly and inefficient and breaks down more quickly than one that is centered. The centered wheel moves forward in a seemingly effortless way, making progress in an orderly and efficient manner. George Matheson speaks of this richer, fuller life and its source in his prayer poem, the first stanza of which is:

> O love that wilt not let me go,
> I rest my weary soul in thee;
> I give thee back the life I owe,
> That in thine ocean depths its flow
> May richer, fuller be.

Notice that he speaks of giving back the weary life and receiving in its place the richer, fuller life our souls, minds, and bodies long for.

John Greenleaf Whittier says it another way,

> Take from our souls the strain and stress,
> And let our ordered lives confess
> The beauty of thy peace.

This is a relationship that can only be hinted at in a book of this sort. But from it will flow the order and beauty we seek.

18

FINDING ORDER
IN BEAUTY

RIDING DOWN THE EXPRESSWAY to work on an early spring morning in South Florida can be a wonderful experience, as it was this morning. In front of me to the east the sun was breaking through the clouds that had gathered ahead of me. Heated by the warm Gulf Stream they billowed high, catching the rays of the tropical sun as it rose through the clouds. Beside me, on the flat fields bordering the road, white ground fog, like clouds clinging to earth, hovered above the cool fields. It was like driving through a field of ghost bushes.

I knew the experience was but for a moment. The ground fog was no match for the power of the sun. It would soon yield to the warm rays and everything would be bright and warm again. The moisture of the fog would not actually disappear. It would just be absorbed by the surrounding warmer air.

That is the way it is with Messies. The characteristics that make us Messies don't disappear when we change. We are still forgetful, distractible, sentimental, and all of those other things. But those characteristics cease to be noticeable or influential when they are absorbed by a stronger force, the desire for order and beauty.

Messies love to be involved in creating beauty. Many draw or paint. Others write poetry, children's stories, and fiction. Messies sew, work on crafts, braid rugs, and make hand-dipped candles. Some learn cake decorating or flower arranging.

But you would never guess it from looking at their houses. "Unattractive" is a kind way to describe them. If you look closely, however, you see that the house does have attractive spots. But the beauty of these small places hardly has any effect on the overall drabness of the house. There are nice details, but the framework of beauty is missing.

Many Messies are puzzled as to why their houses don't look nicer after they have worked so hard to supply these fine additions, so they enroll in another craft class or buy another knickknack. Yet somehow the desire for beauty is not satisfied.

Why is beauty so important? Why do our souls yearn for it? What is beauty anyway?

Beauty is that which strikes the senses in such a way as to bring joy, happiness, or pleasure. On seeing a rainbow, Wordsworth felt joy:

My heart leaps up when I behold a rainbow in the sky.

About a field of daffodils he wrote,

And then my heart with pleasure fills and dances with the daffodils.

What joy he described! And what was its source? Beauty. That's what we want from our houses. We want our hearts to leap with joy and to dance in the delight of what we have created. We want others to be pulled into our homes with the lure of loveliness.

But Messies' houses don't do that. They repulse and discourage people from entering. Messie houses are not a source of joy.

God created beauty with our pleasure in mind. When He planted a garden He created a tree with two characteristics. It was pleasant to the eye and good for food. It was both decorative and practical.

Practicality is the greatest enemy of beauty.

Messies have been told so often to "be practical" that they begin to think their appreciation for beauty is wrong. This is a costly mistake. We have a deep need for beauty. Without it we cannot be fulfilled, nor can we get the practical aspects of our lives to fall into place.

Unfortunately the attractive and the practical are frequently at war in the Messie's life, and the practical usually wins.

Practicality, as I said previously, is the greatest enemy of beauty. For example, a Messie may find a desk that has a lot of storage space. It is secondhand, too large for the room, too dark, and doesn't match the rest of the room. But it is such a good price, and so practical. So the ugly, oversized piece enters the room, welcomed excitedly by its proud new owner who has only a vague feeling that something is not quite right. Practicality has won.

Since trying to achieve visual beauty can frustrate Messies, they compensate. They tune out the overview of the room and concentrate on small spots. They gaze contentedly at the pot of spring tulips on the living room table, even though the room around them is graceless.

Another way Messies seek beauty in a drab house is by substituting beautiful words and thoughts for visual beauty. They keep piles of books and magazines around them, frequently in their bedrooms and on the bed. They are pleased to have this much intellectual beauty at their fingertips. But this type of beauty, though important, cannot substitute for the beauty that comes only through our eyes.

Beauty is the mystery and charm created whenever pleasure is mixed in the visual world. This mystery flows from the spirit of the person who creates it and in turn nourishes her spirit as well as the spirits of those with whom she shares her creation. This is what we want in our houses—mystery, beauty, pleasure, nourishment. This can be ours. No more make-do utilitarian living quarters. Beauty can flow from our spirits into our homes, bringing joy to all who enter.

But we must first let go of our "practicality above all" mentality. What we bring into our houses must be beautiful as well as practical. George Santayana, in his classic book on beauty, writes, "A neat plain practical house may have a certain pleasantness but lacks the charm and harmony to enrich us."

When we start our search for gracious surroundings we will feel as though we are walking from the harsh sunlight of a desert into a shaded garden glen. We will experience a sense of balance and coolness. Life will seem more worthwhile, more balanced, and we will feel less tension. When beauty comes to our home we relax and start to see our total surroundings without having to limit our vision to a few pleasant items.

The order that once eluded us is much closer at hand. Messies generally believe that order produces beauty. This is true to some extent. But in the Messie experience I believe it is more true that beauty produces order.

There is one other surprising result of having a beautiful home. Beauty lifts us out of our tiredness and depression. Many people beat the blues by trying on beautiful clothes or walking in a beautiful outdoor setting. Frequently Messies tell me they are bogged down in depression. Part of this depression comes from lack of control, but part comes simply from living in a graceless home.

In *Emotional Phases of a Woman's Life* Jean Lush writes about a woman's need for beauty in this way:

> They somehow recognize the tremendous human need for loveliness. This basic need is often overlooked in our busy lives. We know our basic needs include food, clothing, shelter, and perhaps companionship but seldom consider beauty a necessary item.... Lack of beauty—ugliness—brings grief to the spirit. Shabbiness and disorder drain us.... Beauty creates energy. It lifts the spirit.

Messies work with less energy or dissipated energy because they are worn out by the way the house looks. Depression and listlessness can be overcome by bringing the spark of beauty into the house.

Remember the poems at the beginning of the chapter. Notice the energy words that spring from beauty.

My heart leaps up when I behold a rainbow...

My heart dances with the daffodils.

When was the last time your house brought this kind of energy to you? Don't laugh. It can. Walking into an orderly and beautiful home at the end of a long hard day can give you and your family a new surge of energy. The visual pleasure you experience produces a harmony that will enrich you all. Then begins a wonderful upward spiral. As you are enriched, you are able to bring more beauty to your home, which enriches you further—and on it goes.

So go for it! As you look for order and control, look beyond them to beauty. You will be surprised how much energy it will bring.

Assess the Mess

1. How does your appreciation for beauty affect the orderliness of your life?

   a.

   b.

   c.

   d.

2. List some ideas you have for using the power of beauty to overcome the force of disorderliness.

   a.

   b.

   c.

   d.

Appendix A

MAKEUP MAKE-OVER

FOR MESSIES

THIS IS NOT JUST A BOOK about housekeeping. It's about being nice to ourselves and learning to appreciate beauty.

When our appreciation for beauty returns to our lives, other things begin to improve as well. It has a spillover effect. (Don't worry, you won't have to clean it up.) As we begin to value beauty and see it take shape, we are encouraged to try it in other areas. We feel a sense of pride and joy in what we are. From this new understanding of our own worth and dignity comes the desire to improve our appearance. At least that is what happened to me.

I have always been interested in looking my best and for the most part I think I've succeeded. On a television show in Cleveland, the hostess commented with surprise, "Why, you don't look like a Messie!" I was afraid to ask what she was expecting. Stringy hair? An ill-fitting suit? Unmatched shoes? Surprisingly, Messies are usually able to maintain their personal appearance very well. But they don't look as good as they could. The hassle of getting clean (and matching) clothes, coordinating jewelry and shoes, and who-knows-what-else together at the same time stresses the organizational ability of the hurried Messie.

This carries over to makeup as well. Too much hurry, too many distractions, too little desire, and too little knowledge of how to use makeup keep the improving Messie from using cosmetics to her best advantage.

Taking Stock of What You've Got

If you haven't given much thought to this in the past, your first question is "How do I begin?" You have little or no makeup in your drawer or it is filled with bits and pieces of past glory that is:

(a) too good to throw out.

(b) so old it may have all dried up or become contaminated.

(c) probably the wrong color because it is out of style or not quite right for your complexion.

(d) O.K. but you're not sure you want to use it.

(e) all of the above.

In my case, it was "all of the above." I was in a muddle. One of my New Year's goals had been to improve my appearance. We all tend to imitate the people we are with, and I had had lunch on a regular basis with a tall, dignified woman who always color coordinated her outfits, including her jewelry and makeup. Her example lifted my sights and I began pumping her for information. I also started asking for advice from professional consultants.

Gathering Information

The first approach I took to self-improvement was to go to the drugstore and buy a few cosmetics on a hit-or-miss basis. I was shy about asking for help and drugstore personnel are not generally trained to give it, so I missed about as much as I hit, and I wasted money on products I couldn't use.

When I realized this was not working very well I got a book on improving appearance that had a chapter on makeup. It was very helpful.

This little knowledge gave me the courage to search further. The best thing I did was to go to the beauty counters of department stores and ask about makeup. There I found a world of serious beauty concern. I got down to business myself. They gave me brochures and samples, rubbed their products on my face, neck, and arms, and gave me advice.

On different days, I had my face made up by four different experts. To give helpful advice, an expert must actually see your face to determine your skin type and color. You need to try products to know which are best for you.

The Wonderful World of Cosmetics

Complexion care comes in two parts: skin care and makeup. It is easy to judge how your face looks. It is not easy to judge whether or not a certain skin-care program will change how your skin will look in twenty years, as many claim.

Before we can proceed with makeup, we need to know our skin type. I thought I had oily skin but the consensus among the makeup artists was that I did not. When I told them my nose became oily, they said almost everybody's does. As it turns out, I have combination skin—oily in the middle, dry on the sides. All agreed about my combination skin, which gave me some confidence that they knew what they were doing. One consultant said my skin on the sides was "parched," which was somewhat alarming. Her line of products was heavy into care for dry skin.

They spoke of facials and products "just as good as a facial" that I could use at home. They spoke of protecting the skin from the sun, computer rays, rays from fluorescent lighting, and glare from car windshields. They spoke of wind damage and pollution protection and of how drugstore makeup might clog the pores. They spoke of honey, almond, and all-natural ingredients. One consultant said that her product had been judged by the FDA as "the closest thing to cosmetic surgery." They spoke of hypoallergenic products. They spoke of repairing damaged cells. I had heard a report on the unsubstantiated claims of cosmetic companies about anti-aging products, but I guess the beauty consultants had not heard it because they spoke of that too.

There is a lot of illusion in the cosmetic world on both sides of the counter. Women want to dream and believe there is magic somewhere in a bottle. If the product they buy makes them feel better about their appearance then it has been partially successful. I am not saying that misrepresentation is excusable. I am simply saying that we should take some of the claims as more hope than fact.

One thing we do know for sure is that skin needs moisture. We all need to drink at least eight glasses of water a day. We also need to seal our skin with moisturizer to keep the moisture from evaporating. I used to think moisturizer would make my skin more oily, but moisturizer is non-greasy and keeps the water, not the oil, inside the skin where it belongs. Apply moisturizer after you bathe to seal in the moisture, every evening after removing makeup, and every morning before putting it on. Moisturizer helps your base go on more evenly and protects your pores from makeup and pollutants. Many moisturizers also have a sunscreen that protects against harmful rays, a mortal enemy of healthy skin.

Rose Kennedy has carried an old-fashioned habit through her many years of life. She always wears a hat with a brim to shield her face from the sun. As it turns out, she was far ahead of her time. Living in Florida where sun damage is a very real threat, not only because it ages the skin but also because it causes skin cancer, we are constantly warned by dermatologists not to expose our skin to the sun. But at the beach day after day thousands do. Sooner or later, the skin will suffer because of it.

As I was talking to the beauty consultant who told me my skin was parched, she whispered to me, "The secret to having moist, youthful skin is to buy a bottle of Evian mineral water at the store and spray it on your face with a spritz bottle just before you put on your moisturizer." She looked around and leaned closer, gesturing toward the other cosmetic consultants behind their counters. "None of these others will tell you that. But it's true." As a final parting word she said, "You can buy it at most discount stores." Because I had read something similar in two other books, I believed her.

I live in the only subtropical area in the United States, south Florida. (California is considered Mediterranean in climate.) It is very humid here and we don't use heat in our houses, so we do not have to worry about lower humidity in the house in the winter. That is not true of most places in the country, however. If you have to heat your house, buy a humidifier, boil water on the stove, put water near the heat source, or do something to replace the moisture in the air. Sleep with a humidifier in your room. You probably know a hundred other things to do. It has been years since I lived in northern Indiana, and I have forgotten most of what I knew about the problem.

Getting the Canvas Ready

Before you put on any makeup you need to be sure your face is ready for it. The first three steps should be done twice a day: before putting on makeup and after removing it.

Get It Clean!

To clean your skin use one of the many cleaning products available from a department store or drugstore. If you go to the drugstore, read the labels well because each product is for a certain kind of skin. Lubriderm is a popular cleanser available in the drugstore. If you are used to a facial cleansing bar (i.e., soap) there are many of these available as well. The cleanser will gather up the pollution, dirt, excess oil, old makeup, and dead skin cells. Put the cleanser on your face with your fingers and circle gently. Rinse well with handfuls of water and pat dry. For the eyes, use a special makeup removal solvent. It is very gentle for the sensitive eye area.

Get It Cleaner Still!

After you have cleansed the skin, use a toner to whisk away any soil or cleanser that might remain. These may also be called freshener, astringent, or facial rinse. Each is designed for a certain type of skin, so read the labels. Toners for oily skin have more alcohol than the toners for dryer skin.

Keep It Moist

While the skin is still moist from cleansing, apply moisturizer to seal it in. Moisturizer also helps the makeup base go on more smoothly.

One Final Step

Once or twice a week or whenever you happen to think of it (Messies tend to lose track of time on things like this) give yourself a good facial scrub or masque to clean away deep-down oil and dirt and to remove dead skin cells. Like all cleansing of the face and neck, do it gently. (Do not include the eyes in this or any other cleansing of the face since the eye area is very delicate and needs special treatment.) Use cotton balls or a facial sponge to remove the masque and rinse with water to remove. At this time the skin especially needs an application of moisturizer to protect it. Now your face is refreshed, toned, and ready to glow.

The Tools You Need

Tools is such a masculine word, let's call them "magic wands" instead; makeup is a romantic and fun kind of thing.

1. **Big Fat Brush**. The first magic wand you will need is a big sable brush to use for putting on loose powder. It may cost a lot but it will last forever and you can leave it to your children when you die. Some people say that you can use your husband's old shaving brush. This is true. But I hate to see you using this make-do attitude so common to frugal Messies. You really do need a makeup brush designed for this purpose.

2. **A Really Good Tweezer**. (Not one you have been using to remove ingrown toenails and have bent so badly that now it only works half the time and then not well.)

3. **Makeup Sponges**. You can buy these anywhere. They come in bunches. They are triangular. You use them for putting on makeup, concealer, etc.

4. **Cotton Swabs**. These are used for removing smudges, blending, and removing your masque or eye makeup. Avoid using tissues. They are rougher than cotton balls. You may wish to have some cotton swabs on hand for blending eye makeup.

5. **Makeup Mirror**. You need a place with a good mirror and a good light together. If you don't have a mirror located in a well-lighted area, buy one that sits on a stand so you can take it to a bright place to work, preferably near a window where you can take advantage of natural light. If you are half blind, as I seem to be becoming, and you have to take off your glasses to put on makeup, you need a magnifying mirror as a part of your makeup mirror.

6. **Extras**. You may wish to get an eyelash curler and a mister or atomizer for squirting on the mineral water I mentioned earlier. Some people would say these too are necessities. I will let you be the judge of that.

7. More stuff. You will need more brushes and small foam-tipped applicators, but these are frequently included in the blush and the eye-shadow packages when you buy them. Finally you will need a pencil sharpener to sharpen your eyebrow pencil, your eyeliner pencil, and your lip-liner pencil if you get any of these. The pencil sharpener is sometimes included with the pencils. If one is not included with the pencil you buy, they are available in drugstores.

The Paint Itself

You don't need a lot of makeup to look beautiful. You do need the right makeup. Don't get rid of your leftover makeup until you know what you really need. However, be mentally prepared to get rid of it if you see that it is not perfect for you. Now is not the time to refuse to throw away stuff because you may find some use for it someday. We are going for perfection here. We want you to be special.

Copy the list of products I have mentioned here to take with you as you go comparison shopping, which you need to do before laying out a penny of your money. You will need to go to a beauty consultant to find out about your skin type, color, etc. Department store makeup artists, cosmetic store consultants, or at-home consultants will be very willing to give you all the advice you ask for. Many will schedule an appointment for a make-over for you. Usually it is without obligation but sometimes it is with a minimum purchase. Ask if there is a minimum purchase required for the make-over. They will advise you as to skin care for your type of skin. Some will give a facial. They will put on the base they choose for you, tell you what kind of blush they advise and what color eye shadow. You will walk away with a good idea of what that product can do for you. Do not feel obligated to buy from them until you are sure. Tell them, as I did, that you have decided to upgrade your makeup and that you are trying out various lines to find which is best for you. Tell them you are trying several before deciding. Don't be shy and never let a salesperson pressure you to make a decision. One of the products you try will be just right for you. Wait until you find it before you buy.

There are many promotional giveaways in cosmetic marketing. By keeping your eyes open for ads you will be able to get some of these additional gifts with your purchases.

1. **The Foundation or Base.** This is the most important part of the makeup. You should choose the kind necessary for coverage and the color that is right for you. If you have clear, beautiful skin you will need sheer coverage. For a natural look, use the sheerest you can get by with. Use oil-base foundation for dry skin and water-base foundation for oily skin. All fair complexions have either yellow or pink undertones. The base you choose needs to have the same undertones and should match the color of your complexion as nearly as possible. To tell if your foundation matches your skin tone, test it by placing a stripe at your jawline. That's where your skin's truest undertones show through. The right shade will almost disappear. If your base doesn't match your natural color as exactly as possible you will have a line at your chin and jaw where your makeup stops. You will look made-up in the poorest sense of the word.

Brown or black complexions need special consultations because these complexions may also have blue undertones. There are some excellent product lines and consultants for black women in many department stores. Many blush and eye-shadow colors work well for both dark and fair complexions, but there are some colors that look great only on dark complexions and are not available except in black-oriented cosmetic lines. If you have a dark complexion and have been getting nice products from general cosmetic lines, go to a line especially for black women and you may find you have been overlooking a whole array of lovely colors not available elsewhere.

2. **Concealer.** This comes in liquid, cream, or stick. Liquid is best.

3. **Powder Blushes.** Two or three are enough.

4. **Loose Translucent Powder.**

5. **Eye Shadows.** Four will do.

6. **Eyeliner Pencil.**

7. **Lip Liner.**

8. **Lipstick.**

9. **Mascara.**

There are other cosmetics you may want to get but we will mention these as we go along. Remember, it is your choice whether these are expensive or inexpensive. Whatever you get will probably be more than is in your makeup budget right now. So take it easy and add as you go.

The Beauty Begins

Makeup is fun stuff. Styles change with the seasons and mood of fashions. New products come out. Even those who know a lot about makeup need to keep up with the changes. While I was getting a facial at a counter in a department store, a very attractively dressed woman came to the counter to see the latest spring colors in eye shadows. (They were expected in the next day. The beauty consultant said a lot of people had been calling to see if they were in yet. Do you believe that people call department stores to get the latest in eye-shadow colors!) As the makeup artist continued my transformation and gave me tips, the woman I thought had it all together came over to ask if she could watch and get some tips on how to improve her makeup. I suppose we are all novices in some ways. Those of us who are just learning are not all that different from many people who have been at it for years.

Now that your face is clean and moisturized and you have assembled the products you need, let's go!

1. Put on the makeup base using either your fingers or the makeup sponge. I think a damp sponge is much better. Smooth it evenly over the face, paying special attention to the lines of your jaw, chin, and hair. Blend it evenly and gently. Don't worry if it gets on your lips. That will just help set your lipstick later.

2. Dot the concealer on any blemishes—spidery veins, dark spots, or dark under-eyes—that may show through the base you have applied. Don't rub it in. Just touch it on lightly with your finger. Too much concealer or too much rubbing will only exaggerate the imperfection.

3. Cheek color comes next. Locate your cheekbones with your fingers. In a kidney shape, from the cheekbone just below the center of the eye at its widest point and curving just up to the temple at its narrowest point, add powder color that complements your makeup and the clothes you are wearing. Blend it in gently

until it looks as though the glow is part of your own cheek. Dot a gentle touch of color on the tip of the nose and on the chin and blend in till it looks like a natural part of your glow.

Although many blushes come in sets of two with the instructions to contour with the darker color, I don't recommend it as a regular thing. A simple one-color blush seems to look nicest.

Another good hint to remember is to put cream rouge on before the powder blush because the cream lasts longer.

4. Eye color is an area where a person's own distinctive style stands out and where fashion changes show up first. Teenagers just starting out do strange and wonderful things with eye makeup. They can play with makeup and get away with it. Most women, however, want eye shadow to enhance their eyes while looking natural. Skill and practice are required to do this.

The eyeliner should be put on with a pencil that matches your eye shadow. Some people line the whole eye with the pencil. Many who wish to make their eyes look more natural and larger run the pencil only from the center of the bottom lid to just beyond the outer corner. The more completely you outline your eye, the smaller it tends to look. It is very important to get very close to the lashes, that is, to draw the line just above the lash line on the upper lid and just below the lashes on the bottom. Leave no space between the pencil mark and the lashes.

There are two ways to get a softer look than that achieved by an eyeliner pencil. The first one is to use the point of the sponge applicator dipped into brown or gray eye shadow to outline the eye. Then soften the line with a clean cotton swab. Some women who use eyeliner pencil put this additional eye shadow powder line over the eyeliner pencil to soften the look of the pencil. Another way to outline the eyes is by dampening a small pointed eyeliner brush and dipping it into the brown or gray eye-shadow powder. Get enough color on the brush to make a thin line just above and below the lash line. This too gives a more subtle look than the eyeliner pencil.

5. Translucent powder sets the makeup you have on. It gives you a finished look and also protects your face from grime and pollution. Translucent powder is not strongly tinted to have its own color. It reflects the color you have on. It does not go on over eye

makeup. Put loose translucent powder on with that fat makeup brush I mentioned earlier. Dust off excess powder with cotton balls or a soft powder puff. Don't worry if it gets on your lips. Lipstick will go on over it and stay on better because of it.

6. Don't forget the eyebrows. To make them look their nicest, be sure they are plucked nicely following their natural line but eliminating any stray hairs. If your brows look spotty you may wish to fill them in or darken them. For dark brows that need to be filled in, use a sharp pencil the color of your brows. Make short feathery lines like hairs where there are gaps in the brow. Don't paint a brow on your face. This looks fake. Just fill in as little as necessary to get the best look. Older women may wish to fill gaps in softly with a very lightly dusted sponge applicator and pale brown shadow instead of the harsher pencil lines. Finish by brushing the eyebrows with a brow brush or an extra toothbrush. Do the brows after the powder to remove the excess powder that drops on them.

7. At last we come to the lips. First line your lips with lip liner. This keeps the color from bleeding or feathering onto your face. It gives a much more finished look. The lip liner does not have to match your lipstick exactly but it needs to be in the same color family. Blend the line softly onto your lips with your little finger so it won't look like you have a line around your lips. Now apply lipstick between the lines. Use the lipstick directly from the stick or use a lipstick brush. If you wish, add a spot of gloss to the center of your bottom lip for interest or, as one beauty consultant told me, "for that pouty look."

8. Finally, the finishing touches. I put these touches last because they are optional with me. The first is curling the lashes with a lash curler. The second is putting on mascara. Mascara comes in two forms: mascara that darkens your lashes and mascara that builds up the lashes and makes them appear fuller and longer as it darkens them. There is also waterproof mascara. For better coverage when you put on mascara, let the first application dry and then add another.

I don't like to use mascara because it is so hard to remove and excessive rubbing of the sensitive skin around the eyes can cause damage and loss of elasticity (in other words, bags under the eyes).

Now you know just about everything that I, as a novice, found out about makeup. There are lots of extra things, of course, which you will find out as salespeople tell you of the joys of their products. Just remember to take things slowly as you begin. If you have not been wearing much makeup and decide to upgrade your appearance in this area, don't make the change too abruptly. It will startle both you and your friends.

How much makeup should you wear? Wear as much as you need to protect your face and as much as makes you look nice in the context of your life. Makeup will make you look better, not funnier, if properly applied. People will not ask about your makeup. They will say things like, "My, you look so rested. Have you been on vacation?" Or they will say, "You look different. Did you have your hair cut?" Or simply, "You look nice today."

If you seldom get out because you live in an isolated area or if your friends do not wear much makeup, you still need to care for your skin with cleanser, toner, and masques, and to use moisturizer, base, and powder to protect your skin. A little lipstick and blush won't hurt to perk up your face. The other things can be saved for special occasions.

The Best Source of Beauty

Makeup is only an enhancer. A life balanced between work and play, regular exercise, well-balanced eating, and staying away from bad habits will produce a glow from within that makeup cannot provide.

In college I decided once not to give any attention to my appearance while I gave attention to developing my inner self. But I soon learned that looking dowdy did not improve my inner self. If anything, a frumpy look is a contradiction to the beautiful spirit one wishes to have. Makeup, like many things in life, has to be a part of a larger balanced life-style. There is a certain harmony in having a beautiful spirit and beautiful face to match.

Deeper still is the beauty of the Spirit that shines through the eyes, the bearing, and the personality. The Bible speaks of the beauty of holiness. This beauty is not caused by a halo and a wispy smile. This beauty is the love and joy that come from knowing the God who is love.

Appendix B

SELF-HELP

SUPPORT GROUPS

MESSIES ANONYMOUS support groups are not a homogeneous group. They all exist to help reforming Messies keep on track with their goals, but they all do it in different ways.

Getting Started

There are a variety of ways for Messies Anonymous groups to start. Sometimes two individual Messies will meet, realize their mutual interest, and begin to get together for support and fellowship. Occasionally a women's group in a church or other organization will begin a support group for those who want to concentrate on getting organized. Sometimes an existing group that meets regularly decides to study organization, so they form a temporary Messies Anonymous support group. For you it may be as simple as asking if others in your Sunday school class would like to meet with you in a group. Sometimes one person will catch a vision of how an M.A. group could benefit her personally and the community as well. She will advertise in a local paper for interested persons to call her. Some groups grow as they advertise and function over a long period of time, incorporating new members as they go. Others continue with the original members until their needs are met and then disband.

Although the Messies Anonymous program is not designed to be a twelve-step program, such as Alcoholics Anonymous, if a group wishes to use the twelve-step approach in their Messies Anonymous group they may do so for their own purposes. Frequently those who have been involved in support groups other than Messies Anonymous understand how they work and feel more confident in beginning a group. They will already have a line on which churches, hospitals, or other organizations allow support groups to meet in their facilities. Knowing where to meet is a big step. On the other hand, getting a meeting room is not always necessary. A small group of four or six could meet at a restaurant for lunch. Even if some member has a house neat enough to meet in, it is usually better to hold the meeting in a public place.

Whether or not to use a twelve-step program is up to the group. Unless the whole group is enthusiastic about such a plan, I recommend that you not try to follow the program developed by Alcoholics Anonymous and adopted by various groups. Controversy over the type of group can distract from your goal of recovering your sanity in organized living. The twelve traditions, which are group rules, certainly apply well to any self-help group, including Messies Anonymous. They are readily available in literature from Alcoholics Anonymous and its sister groups. As an alternative to starting a Messies Anonymous twelve-step program, you may wish to attend a twelve-step program such as Adult Children of Alcoholics (ACOA) or go to some of the groups in which the twelve steps are explored in-depth. Those who wish to do so will find it easy to apply the twelve steps to their own addiction to disorder and lack of control over their lives. Chapter 7, "Parenting the Child Within," gives more information to help you determine whether or not a twelve-step program will be useful to you.

The Objectives

The support group has several objectives. The first is encouragement. Being a Messie is very discouraging. If there was one word that described my life as a Messie, it was *frustrating*. Many women have said with relief, "I thought I was the only one." Sometimes by the time Messies get to the first support group meeting they have developed a great deal of confusion and discouragement about the problem and their inability to control it.

The second goal is motivation. The focus Messies need to rightly order their lives and homes is kept sharper by talking regularly about successes of the last week and goals for the coming week. Those who come to the meeting are encouraged to write their goals for the coming week. In that way they make them more specific. The commitment is stronger. They are also encouraged to tell of their successes of the last week. To make sure each person has the opportunity to do both—tell of past successes and set future goals—members of larger support groups will need to break up into smaller groups to make sure they have time. Hearing of others' successes, telling our own, and setting specific goals act as powerful motivation for the Messie.

The final goal of the support group is to offer information. The group may read an article or part of a book on an appropriate subject. They may each read a paragraph and make comments as they go. They may have one member review a chapter of a book about household organization or cleaning. They may have a member tell the story of how she met the problem and solved it. On some occasions an outsider might speak to the group. After the meeting more informal sharing will take place.

Although Messies Anonymous support groups do not endorse any particular products or people, members may want to share what has helped them. For instance, it is helpful to know about a product that works well for cleaning bathroom fixtures in an area that has hard water. Someone may have used a cleaning service they are pleased with. All of these come under the heading of information.

Finally, some support groups may want to act as community representatives concerning the problem of disorganization. They may contact the life-style editor of the local newspaper and volunteer information for articles on the subject of household organization. Three particularly good times of the year to suggest these articles are spring, when it is traditional to think about housecleaning; fall, when holiday preparation stresses organizational ability in the home; or at the beginning of the year, when people are thinking about New Year's resolutions.

You will be amazed at the interest shown in stories of people who have overcome the problem of messiness. In addition to your own local and personal input, you may give the Messies Anonymous headquarter's phone number as a resource number for newspaper reporters to call. You may also tell the newspaper that an introductory newsletter on the subject will be sent to readers who write and ask for one. The address and phone number are listed at the end of this book.

The Members

Most who are involved will be women, though men are certainly welcome. Men should probably be more concerned with their own problems of messiness, but nonetheless, the problem falls most heavily on women and they will be the ones to come to a support group.

Since the group consists primarily of women, give some thought as to what to do with children who come with their mothers to the meeting. If the group meets in a church where nursery facilities are available, the problem can be solved by hiring someone to oversee the children while the group is in session. Each group needs to address its own needs as they come up.

The Organization

There are two kinds of organization: informal and formal. Most of the groups will be informal because the reason the members are meeting does not require a lot of structure. A few people will meet together and voluntarily take roles of leadership. Sometimes leadership is rotated among the members. Decisions are made by the leader or by consensus. There are no dues or official membership. Funds are provided as needed by donations or collections. No official bank account is opened. The funds are small and kept in a cookie jar on somebody's kitchen shelf.

More formal groups are usually larger and have a tighter structure. They may charge dues, have a membership list, produce a newsletter, etc. They may elect officers and function by voting on questions.

There is overlap in these two styles. Most women have had enough experience in groups to know what kind they are comfortable with or what kind is common in their area.

Communication

In small groups it is easy to keep in touch by phone between meetings. If the group grows larger, a phone chain is useful for relaying information. Remember, however, that the phone is a big distraction from the work we want to get done. It would be ironic if using the phone for the work of a Messies Anonymous group should interfere with the reason we joined the group to begin with. Use the phone sparingly. Communicate at the meetings.

Some groups may wish to put out a newsletter with articles, poems, announcements, etc. Again, do this only if it does not interfere with the main point of the meeting. If you have to spend too much time putting out the newsletter, the purpose for the group is lost. If you're convinced a newsletter is useful, try preparing it at one of the regular meetings.

For new members, you may wish to have a printed brochure that tells how the group works. If you plan it carefully, you can make this double as a promotional piece for potential members and, with permission, leave several brochures in doctors' offices, on store counters, etc. This depends on how the group sees itself in terms of outreach to the community.

Activities

When a group begins to get into complicated activities, it is going afield of its purpose. With few exceptions, the meetings should not be more than an hour. They should be to the point. The group may wish to begin or close with the prayer of serenity and develop an agenda that they follow consistently. For example,

Welcome
Group Reading of the Purpose
Report on Successes of the Week (in groups of two)
Reading Material or Presentation by Member
Brief Discussion
Serenity Prayer

The group may wish to display books for sale (some may be purchased for group discount from M.A. headquarters) or for lending. If the facilities permit, some refreshments may be served but this should be minimal (unless, of course, you're meeting at a restaurant). On special occasions the group may want to have a potluck meal. Keep it simple and short. Don't let this group or any other group take time from your primary commitment. Use it for your own good. Don't let it use you. That's what Messies Anonymous is all about.

Assess the Mess

1. Would a support group help you meet your goals?
   - ☐ Yes
   - ☐ No
2. If so, how can you begin one if there is not one in your area? (Check as many of the following as may apply.)
   - ☐ A friend can meet with me.
   - ☐ I can form a group from an organization I now belong to.
   - ☐ I can advertise in a local paper, flyer, or on a radio station (frequently they carry public service announcements without charge).
   - ☐ Other
3. When would be a convenient time for you to meet?
   - ☐ Morning
   - ☐ Afternoon
   - ☐ Evening
   - ☐ Other (e.g., over lunch)
4. Where might you meet once your group is started?
   - ☐ A church meeting room
   - ☐ A hospital meeting room
   - ☐ A restaurant
   - ☐ Other

Two can accomplish more than twice as much as one, for the results can be much better. If one falls, the other pulls him up.... Three is even better, for a triple-braided cord is not easily broken (from Ecclesiastes 4:9–12 TLB).

Please rush me my Flipper Kit, a system to help me *keep* my house in order. My check to Messies Anonymous for $17.95 is enclosed for each Flipper Kit. This includes handling and postage.

Name:

Street Address:

City:

State:

Zip:

Phone:

To order valuable services from Sandra Felton, check the following areas of interest:

☐ I would like an introductory newsletter with other helpful hints from Messies Anonymous. (Enclosed is $1.00 for printing, handling, and postage.)

☐ I am interested in having Sandra Felton come and speak in my area for a seminar. My group (if any) is:

☐ I would like to be an M.A. Pen Pal. I have enclosed a 9-inch business-size, stamped, self-addressed envelope.

☐ I am interested in an M.A. Self-Help group in my area. Let me know if there is one already. Send more information about starting one if there is not one already in my area.

Write to:
    Messies Anonymous
    Department M
    5025 SW 114th Avenue
    Miami, Florida 33165

If you do not wish to cut this page from the book, write us a letter or call us at (305) 271-8404.